clean eating
at peacock ridge farm

by Renae Frey
www.peacockridgefarm.com

PEACOCK RIDGE FARM
Look Great. Feel Great. Live Clean.

welcome

Thank you so much for your interest in reading this cookbook. It truly has been a labor of love and I have enjoyed every minute of it. I am so thrilled to share what I've learned with you.

After fifteen years of living in large cities across the United States, I moved back home to the beautiful Pacific Northwest. Surrounded by majestic mountains and rivers teeming with salmon, there truly is no better place to live than here, it's home.

I love having my hands in the dirt, sometimes accompanied by my granddaughter, growing fresh fruits and vegetables; and to serve healthy and great tasting food to my family and friends.

As my husband and I began to age, we noticed that our bodies were changing a lot! We knew that we needed to make some changes. We decided that we wanted to keep our bodies in as good of shape as possible. That meant in addition to keeping our bodies moving, we needed to eat clean foods as much as possible. That means low carb, whole foods. No potatoes, rice, pasta, breads, beans or corn, refined flours or sugars. We also limit any sweets. I knew that if the food didn't taste great and that if we didn't enjoy a variety of foods, we would never stick to the plan.

So, my dream of writing this cookbook was born. I have educated myself about how food affects your body, both positively and negatively. With a few simple swaps, you will be eating clean in no time. I created these recipes to be easy to make, to not require a great deal of time, talent or too many ingredients. If I can make these meals, you can too.

I am so excited to share this book with you.

Blessings to you,
Renae

table of contents

side dishes

cranberry acorn squash

INGREDIENTS:
1 Acorn Squash
1 T. Butter
1 T. Honey
¼ c. Dried Cranberries
¼ c. Sliced almonds

Preheat oven to 400 degrees.

Cut acorn squash in half.

Cut off a bit of the bottom of the squash so that it can sit level in the baking dish.

Scoop out all of the seeds and pulp, poke acorn squash repeatedly with a fork.

Spread butter on to the squash and drizzle with honey.

Bake for 40 minutes or until the acorn squash is tender.

Remove from oven and sprinkle with cranberries and almonds and bake another 10 minutes.

baked tomatoes

INGREDIENTS:

2 large Tomatoes
1 T. Olive oil
Salt
Pepper
½ t. Italian seasoning
½ c. Mozzarella, grated

Preheat oven to 400 degrees.

Cut the top of tomato off.

Score tomato flesh in a cross hatch pattern all the way through the tomato without piercing the tomato skin.

Mix oil and spices and drizzle over tomato, making sure that the oil mixture soaks down into the tomato.

Sprinkle on mozzarella cheese. Bake for 20 minutes or until cheese is melted and golden brown.

candied carrots

INGREDIENTS:
2 C. Baby carrots
4 Dates, pitted and chopped
1 T. Pistachios, chopped
2 T. Butter, melted
Salt and pepper to taste

Preheat oven to 375 degrees.

Combine all ingredients.

Put into a baking dish and bake for 20-30 minutes or until carrots are fork tender.

cauliflower rice pilaf

INGREDIENTS:
1 Head cauliflower, grated finely
1 T. Coconut oil
8 Dried apricot halves, chopped
1 ½ T. Raisins
2 T. Pistachios, chopped
½ Onion, chopped finely
1 t. Garlic, minced
½ t. Cumin
½ t. Cinnamon
Salt
Pepper

In a large pan, heat coconut oil.

Add garlic and onions and sauté until tender.

Add all other ingredients and cook until cauliflower is cooked through.

curry & coconut cauliflower

INGREDIENTS:
2 T. Olive oil
1 Cauliflower, cut into florets
¼ t. Salt
¼ t. Pepper
½ t. Curry
½ c. Cashews, chopped
½ c. Cranberries
¼ c. Coconut, shredded

Preheat oven to 400 degrees.

Mix all ingredients in a large bowl. Spread onto a baking sheet.

Bake for 40 minutes or until cauliflower is tender.

cilantro cauliflower rice

INGREDIENTS:
1 Head of cauliflower, grated
1 T. Coconut oil
Salt and pepper to taste
¼ c. Fresh cilantro, finely chopped
½ t. Cayenne
2 T. Coconut milk

In a large pan, heat oil.

Add cauliflower, salt, pepper, cilantro and cayenne.

Cook until cauliflower becomes transparent.

Add coconut milk.

cumin roasted carrots

INGREDIENTS:

1 lb. Carrots
½ T. Cumin
¼ t. Cinnamon
Salt
Pepper
1 ½ t. Coconut oil
Parsley

Preheat oven to 400 degrees.

Put all ingredients into a large Ziploc bag and shake until well mixed.

Put carrots on a baking sheet.

Bake for 20 minutes or until carrots are crisp tender but not soft.

green beans almandine

INGREDIENTS:
1 Lb. Fresh Green Beans
3 c. Chicken broth
2 T. Butter
½ c. Almonds, sliced
Salt and Pepper to taste

In a double boiler, steam green beans with the chicken broth.

Cook until green beans are tender. Drain.

Add butter, almonds, salt and pepper.

green beans & tomatoes

INGREDIENTS:

1½ lbs. Fresh green beans
¼ c. Onions, diced
2 c. Chicken stock
1 T. Butter
1 t. Garlic, minced
Salt
Pepper
5 strips Bacon, cooked, crumbled
1 Large tomato, diced

In a double boiler, steam green beans in the chicken stock, just until green beans are tender, but not soft.

Drain green beans and set aside. In a large pan, sauté onions and garlic in butter until soft and golden.

Add salt, pepper, bacon, tomatoes and green beans and cook until flavors are well mixed.

grilled asparagus

INGREDIENTS:
1 Bunch fresh asparagus
1 T. Butter
½ t. Garlic, minced
Salt
Pepper

In a pan, melt butter.

Add garlic and asparagus and cook just until tender.

Salt and pepper to taste.

honey glazed butternut squash

INGREDIENTS:
½ Butternut squash, diced
¼ c. Water
2 T. Butter
1 T. Honey

Put butternut squash and water in a microwave safe bowl.

Microwave squash for 12-15 minutes until squash is tender. Drain.

Add butter and honey to butternut squash. Mix well.

honey glazed carrots

INGREDIENTS:
4 c. Baby carrots
2 c. Chicken stock
1 T. Butter
1 T. Honey
Pinch of Parsley

Cook carrots in chicken stock until carrots are tender, but not soft.

Drain off chicken stock.

Add butter and honey, mix well.

Sprinkle with parsley.

loaded sweet potatoes

INGREDIENTS:
4 Small sweet potatoes
1 T. Olive oil
¼ c. Almond milk
Dash Salt
Dash Pepper
1 C. Cheddar cheese, grated
½ c. Bacon, cooked, crumbled
1 t. Chives

Preheat oven to 400 degrees.

Wash sweet potatoes. Pierce sweet potatoes with a fork several times. Rub with olive oil. Bake sweet potatoes for 45 minutes or until potatoes are tender.

Cut sweet potatoes in half lengthwise. Scoop out half of the sweet potato flesh and put it in a small bowl.

Put potato skins back in the oven for 10 minutes.

Meanwhile, combine sweet potato flesh with almond milk, salt, pepper and chives.

Fill potato skins with the filling and top with cheese and bacon.
Bake until cheese melts.

mashed cauliflower

INGREDIENTS:
I Large cauliflower, cut into florets
3 c. Chicken stock
1 t. Garlic, minced
1 T. Butter
½ c. Coconut milk
Salt
Pepper
Chives

Boil cauliflower in chicken stock until tender.

Drain cauliflower.

Add garlic, butter, coconut milk, salt and pepper.

Blend until cauliflower is smooth.

Sprinkle on chives.

mashed sweet potatoes

INGREDIENTS:

4 Large sweet potatoes, diced
2 c. Chicken stock
4 T. Butter
1 c. Almond milk
1 t. Ground ginger
1 t. Cinnamon, ground
¼ t. Salt

In a large saucepan, steam sweet potatoes in the chicken stock, just until tender, but not too soft. Drain.

Add butter, almond milk, ginger, cinnamon and salt.

Whip sweet potatoes until smooth.

baked parmesan zucchini

INGREDIENTS:

½ t. Basil, dried
¼ t. Garlic powder
½ t. Oregano
2 t. Parsley
½ t. Thyme
4 small Zucchini, quartered lengthwise
Salt
Pepper
1 T. Olive oil
½ c. Parmesan cheese

Preheat oven to 400 degrees.

Spray a baking dish with olive oil spray. Set aside.

In a large Ziploc bag, add basil, garlic, oregano, parsley, thyme, salt, pepper, olive oil and Parmesan cheese.

Shake until well mixed.

Add zucchini; shake until zucchini is well coated.

Bake for 20-25 minutes.

roasted butternut squash

INGREDIENTS:
1 Butternut squash, diced
1 T. Olive oil
Salt and pepper
1 T. Butter
¼ c. Cranberries, dried
¼ c. Almonds, chopped
1 T. Maple syrup

Preheat oven to 400 degrees.

Line a baking sheet with parchment paper.

In a large bowl, mix butternut squash, olive oil, salt and pepper. Arrange butternut squash onto the baking sheet.

Bake butternut squash for 30-45 minutes, or until butternut squash is tender.

In a large bowl, mix roasted butternut squash, butter, cranberries, almonds and maple syrup.

parmesan roasted cauliflower

INGREDIENTS:

2 T. Olive oil

1 Head Cauliflower, cut into florets

Salt

Pepper

1 t. Garlic, minced

¼ c. Parmesan cheese, grated

Mix all ingredients in a large bowl until well mixed.

Put on a cookie sheet and bake at 400 degrees, turning cauliflower often, until cauliflower is golden brown.

roasted spaghetti squash

INGREDIENTS:
1 Spaghetti Squash
2 T. Butter
Salt
Pepper

Preheat oven to 400 degrees.

Cut spaghetti squash in half, scoop out all seeds and pulp.

Pierce spaghetti squash with a fork repeatedly.

Place spaghetti squash cut side down onto baking sheet. Bake for 45 minutes or until squash is tender.

Using the tines of a fork, pull spaghetti squash into shreds and put into a bowl.

Add butter and salt and pepper to taste. Mix well.

sauteed asparagus & mushrooms

INGREDIENTS:

1 T. Olive oil

1 T. Ginger

1 T. Garlic, minced

2 Bunches of asparagus, chopped

2 c. Mushrooms, sliced

Salt

Pepper

1 T. Soy sauce
  or Coconut aminos

Heat pan over medium heat, add olive oil, ginger and garlic and sauté for 1 minute.

Add asparagus, mushrooms, salt and pepper, cook until vegetables are tender but not soft. Add soy sauce.

tomato bruschetta

INGREDIENTS:
2 Large tomatoes, sliced
1 t. Garlic, minced
¼ c. Almond flour
¼ c. Parmesan cheese
Salt
Pepper
½ T. Olive oil

Preheat oven to 400 degrees.

Line a baking sheet with parchment paper.

Place tomatoes on the baking sheet.

Mix garlic, almond flour, parmesan cheese, salt, pepper and
olive oil.

Put the mixture onto the tomatoes.

Bake for 15 minutes or until topping is golden brown.

zucchini & squash au gratin

INGREDIENTS:

2 medium Zucchini, sliced
2 medium Yellow squash, sliced
1 T. Olive oil
1 t. Garlic, minced
¼ c. Onion, finely chopped
¼ t. Salt
¼ t. Pepper
½ pint Heavy cream
½ c. Parmesan cheese, grated
1 T. Arrowroot powder
2 T. Water

Preheat oven to 400 degrees. Oil Baking dish, set aside.

In a saucepan, add oil, garlic, onion, salt and pepper; cook until onions are tender.

Add heavy cream and parmesan cheese, cook until boiling. Reduce heat.

Mix together water and arrowroot powder until smooth, add to cream mixture; cook until sauce thickens.

Layer squash and sauce into baking dish.

Bake 40 minutes or until bubbling and golden brown.

appetizers
&
snacks

almond flour biscuits

INGREDIENTS:
2 c. Almond flour
1 t. Baking soda
1 t. Xanthan gum
1 t. Salt
2 ½ T. Butter, cold, diced in small chunks
3 Eggs, beaten

Preheat oven to 400 degrees.

Line a baking sheet with parchment paper.

Mix flour, baking soda, xanthan gum and salt.

Cut in butter.

Add eggs; mix well.

Drop biscuits by spoonfuls onto the baking sheet. Bake for 17-20 minutes.

bacon wrapped pineapple

INGREDIENTS:
2 c. Fresh Pineapple chunks
About 24 Pecan halves
12 Strips Bacon, cut in half

Preheat oven to 350 degrees.

Put a piece of parchment paper onto a baking sheet. Set aside.

Lay out a strip of bacon, layer with pineapple and pecan.

Roll bacon around the pineapple and secure with a toothpick.

Repeat until all pineapple and bacon are used.

Put pineapple onto the baking sheet. Bake for 10-15 minutes.

cauliflower breadsticks

INGREDIENTS:
1 Head cauliflower, grated
2 Eggs
1 c. Cheese, divided
½ t. Garlic powder
½ t. Basil
½ t. Oregano
½ t. Parsley
Dash Salt
Dash Pepper
1 c. Almond flour
1 T. Xanthan gum

Preheat oven to 450 degrees.

Line a baking sheet with parchment paper.

In a glass bowl, microwave cauliflower for 10 minutes.
Drain any excess liquid.

In a large mixing bowl, add all ingredients, except 1/2
c. cheese.
Mix well.

Put dough onto the baking sheet and smooth out.

Bake for 15 minutes. Then top with remaining
cheese.
Bake another 5 minutes.

Bread tends to stay together better if you let it cool
before cutting. Serve with marinara sauce.

sweet asian chicken strips

INGREDIENTS:
4 Chicken breasts, cut into strips
½ c. Sweet chili sauce
½ c. Soy sauce
1 t. Sesame oil
  or Coconut aminos
1 t. Garlic, minced
1 t. Ginger, minced
1 T Cilantro, dried
1 T. Coconut oil

In a Ziploc bag, add sweet chili sauce, soy sauce, sesame oil, garlic, ginger and cilantro. Mix well.

Add chicken and let marinade for ½ hour.

In a large pan, melt coconut oil.

Cook chicken until no longer pink.

coconut almonds

INGREDIENTS:
1 c. Coconut
2 c. Almonds
2 t. Honey

In a frying pan, toast coconut.

Add almonds and honey.

Cook until almonds are well coated and honey starts to harden.

coconut chicken strips

INGREDIENTS:

1 c. Coconut oil

2 Lbs. Chicken breasts, cut into strips

1 c. Coconut, shredded

2 Eggs, beaten

½ c. Coconut milk

2 c. Almond flour

Salt

Pepper

In a large pan, heat coconut oil.

In a small dish, add coconut.

In another small dish, add eggs and coconut milk.

In a third small dish, add almond flour, salt and pepper.

Dip chicken in eggs, then in flour mixture, then in coconut.
Cook in hot oil until golden brown. Serve with sweet chili sauce.

cucumber rollups

INGREDIENTS:
1 Large Cucumber, sliced
lengthwise
Sliced Turkey
Cheddar cheese, sliced
Lettuce
Tomatoes
Honey mustard dressing

Lay out a slice of cucumber and layer turkey, cheese, lettuce, tomato and dressing.

Roll up and secure with a toothpick.

deviled eggs

INGREDIENTS:

12 Eggs, cooked and peeled
½ c. Mayonaise
1 T. Golden mustard
¼ c. Bacon, cooked, crumbled
1 T. Honey
Salt
Pepper
Paprika
Chives

Cut eggs in half, remove yolks.

In a small bowl, combine egg yolks, mayonnaise, mustard, honey, salt and pepper. Blend until smooth. Add bacon, mix well.

Fill egg whites with egg mixture.

Sprinkle with chives and paprika.

garlic sweet chili meatballs

INGREDIENTS:

Meatballs:
1 T. Coconut oil
2 Eggs, beaten
1 ¼ lb. Ground turkey
1 T. Cilantro, dried
½ T. Garlic, minced
½ T. Ginger, minced
½ c. Almond flour
Salt
Pepper

Sauce:
¼ c. Soy sauce
  or Coconut animos
½ t. Garlic, minced
¼ c. Sweet chili sauce
½ t. Lime juice

Heat coconut oil in a large pan.

Mix all meatball ingredients until well combined.

Scoop meatballs with an ice cream scoop and roll into balls.

Cook meatballs on all sides until meatballs are no longer pink.
Set meatballs aside.

In the same pan, add all sauce ingredients.

Cook until sauce starts to thicken. Add meatballs and combine with the sauce.

prosciutto asparagus

INGREDIENTS:
12 Stalks Asparagus
12 Slices prosciutto

Preheat oven to 400 degrees.

Wrap each stalk of asparagus with one slice of prosciutto.

Place on baking sheet. Bake for 15 minutes, or until asparagus is
crisp tender.

shrimp pineapple skewers

INGREDIENTS:

2 c. Fresh pineapple chunks
1 lb. Shrimp, deveined, peeled
¼ c. Sweet chili sauce
¼ c. Hoisin sauce
1 t. Garlic, minced
1 t. Ginger, minced
1 T. Sesame seeds
½ t. Sesame oil
Salt
Pepper

Preheat the grill. Soak wooden skewers in water for 15 minutes. Drain.

In a small saucepan, combine sweet chili sauce, hoisin sauce, garlic, ginger, sesame seeds, sesame oil and salt and pepper.
Cook 10 minutes.

Using the wooden skewers, alternate a piece of pineapple with one shrimp, until skewer is ¾ of the way full.

After using all pineapple and shrimp, place the skewers on the grill. Brush with the sauce.

Cook for about 3 minutes, then turn the skewers over and cook on the other side. Brush with the sauce.

Skewers are done when the shrimp are pink.

snack mix

INGREDIENTS:

1 c. Cashews
½ c. Sunflower seeds
½ c. Dried cherries
½ c. Raisins
½ c. Shredded coconut

In a medium bowl mix all ingredients.

spaghetti squash fritters

INGREDIENTS:
1 T. Olive oil
2 Eggs, beaten
1/3 c. Almond flour
3 c. Spaghetti squash, cooked
1/2 c. Parmesan cheese, grated
1/4 t. Pepper
1/4 t. Salt
Dash crushed red pepper flakes
Dash chives
1/4 c. Bacon, crumbled

Heat oil in pan.

Mix all remaining ingredients, except oil, until well blended.

Drop by spoonfuls into hot oil.

Cook on each side until golden brown.

spicy cashews

INGREDIENTS:

½ lb. Cashews

¼ c. Coconut oil

1 T. Rosemary

1 t. Salt

2 t. Paprika

½ t. Pepper

In a small saucepan, add all ingredients.

Cook until cashews are heated through and nuts are well coated.

stuffed mushrooms

INGREDIENTS:
8 oz. Mushrooms, stems removed
1 ½ c. Sausage
½ T. Coconut cream, unsweetened
½ c. Parmesan cheese
Dash Salt, pepper and garlic

Preheat oven to 400 degrees.

In a medium bowl, combine sausage, coconut cream, Parmesan cheese and spices. Mix well.

Fill mushrooms with the sausage mixture.

Bake for 20 minutes.

sundried tomato bread

INGREDIENTS:

3 c. Almond flour
1 T. Xanthan gum
1 t. Baking soda
1 t. Salt
½ t. Rosemary
½ t. Oregano
½ t. Basil
1 t. Garlic powder
½ c. Sundried tomatoes, chopped
4 Eggs, beaten
1 t. Olive oil

Preheat oven to 350 degrees. Butter a loaf pan.

In a small bowl, mix all dry ingredients.

In another small bowl, mix wet ingredients.

Combine wet and dry ingredients. Pour dough into the loaf pan. Bake for 50-55 minutes.

teriyaki beef skewers

INGREDIENTS:
2 lbs. Beef, sliced into thin strips
½ c. Soy sauce
  or Coconut aminos
½ c. Honey
¼ c. Orange juice
2 T. Rice vinegar
1 T. Ginger, minced
1 T. Garlic, minced
1 T. Sesame oil
⅛ t. Red pepper flakes
¼ t. Sesame seeds
1 t. Water
1 t. Arrowroot powder

In a saucepan, mix soy sauce, honey, orange juice, rice vinegar, garlic, ginger, sesame oil, red pepper flakes. Cook for 5 minutes.

Whisk together water and arrowroot powder.

Add to teriyaki sauce. Simmer until sauce starts to thicken.

Sprinkle in sesame seeds.

Marinate beef in teriyaki sauce for at least 30 minutes.

Thread beef onto skewers. Grill for 5 minutes each side.

greek chicken skewers

INGREDIENTS:
4 Chicken breasts, cut into chunks
1 c. plain Greek yogurt
2 T. Lemon juice
½ t. Oregano
½ t. Cumin
½ t. Paprika
¼ t. Cinnamon
¼ t. Pepper
¼ t. Cardamom
1 t. Salt
2 T. Olive oil
For the sauce:
1 c. Plain Greek yogurt
1 t. Garlic, minced
1 ½ t. Lemon juice
2 T. Onion, finely chopped
½ Cucumber, peeled and grated
1 t. Dried dill weed
½ t. Salt
½ t. Pepper

Soak wooden skewers in water.

In a bowl, mix yogurt, lemon juice, oregano, cumin, paprika, cinnamon, pepper, cardamom, salt and olive oil.

Mix until smooth, add chicken chunks and let marinade at least 15 minutes.

Meanwhile, in a small bowl, mix yogurt, garlic, lemon juice, onion, cucumber, dill weed, salt and pepper.

Slide chicken chunks onto skewers and place on grill.

Cook until golden brown on all sides. Serve with Tzatziti sauce.

zucchini chips

INGREDIENTS:
2 Medium zucchini, sliced
1 T. Olive oil
Salt
Pepper
Dash Cayenne pepper

In a large Ziploc bag, add all ingredients.

Using a food dehydrator, lay zucchini slices in a single layer
on the drying trays.

Dry zucchini for 5 hours or until chips are crisp.

trail mix

INGREDIENTS:

1 c. Almonds
¼ c. Toasted coconut
¼ c. Golden raisins
¼ c. Cherries, dried
¼. C. Macadamia nuts
¼ c. Sunflower seeds

In a medium bowl, mix all ingredients well.

asparagus prosciutto benedict

INGREDIENTS:
16 Asparagus stalks
4 slices prosciutto
4 Eggs
2 t. Apple cider vinegar
2 Scallions, chopped

Hollandaise Sauce:
2 Egg yolks
¼ c. Butter, melted
2 t. Lemon juice
¼ t. Paprika
¼ t. Salt

Pour boiling water in a blender and let stand for 10 minutes.

Trim ends of asparagus. Wrap 4 asparagus stalks with one slice of prosciutto. Grill for 2 minutes on each side or until golden brown.

Meanwhile, poach eggs in water with apple cider vinegar. Place one poached egg on each asparagus bundle.

Empty water out of blender and dry completely. Blend egg yolk, lemon, salt and paprika. With the blender running, slowly pour in melted butter. Blend for 30 seconds.

Pour hollandaise sauce over each poached egg. Top with scallions.

baked eggs in avocados

INGREDIENTS:
2 Avocados
4 Eggs
¼ c. Tomatoes, diced
¼ c. Bacon, cooked, crumbled
1 t. Chives
Salt and pepper

Preheat oven to 350 degrees.

Cut avocados in half; remove seed.

Scoop out some of the flesh, making enough room for the egg.

Put one egg in each avocado half.

Sprinkle with chives, bacon, salt and pepper.

Bake for 20 minutes, or until egg is cooked to your likeness.

Sprinkle with diced tomatoes.

baked eggs in tomato sauce

INGREDIENTS:
1 T. Olive oil
1 t. Garlic, minced
½ T. Dried onion
½ t. Oregano, dried
½ t. Basil, dried
1-15oz. can Petite diced tomatoes
2-15 oz. cans Tomato sauce
Salt
Pepper
6 Eggs
1 c. Mozzarella, grated

Preheat oven to 400 degrees.

Lightly butter baking dish, set aside.

In a large saucepan, add oil, garlic, onion, oregano and basil. Sauté for 2 minutes. Add tomatoes and tomato sauce, cook until sauce thickens.

Pour sauce into baking dish; add eggs and salt and pepper, mozzarella cheese.

Bake for 40 minutes or until eggs are baked.

honey and almond baked pears

INGREDIENTS:
2 Large pears, halved and cored
¼ t. Cinnamon
2 t. Honey
¼ c. Almonds, chopped

Preheat the oven to 350 degrees.

Place the pears, cut side up in a baking dish.

Sprinkle with cinnamon and almonds. Drizzle on honey.

Bake for 30 minutes.

These are great for breakfast or for dessert.

honey bananas

INGREDIENTS:
3 Bananas, sliced
1 T. Butter
½ T. Honey
Dash of Cinnamon

In a pan, melt butter.

Add bananas; cook until bananas start to become golden.

Add honey and dash of cinnamon.

spaghetti squash poached egg

INGREDIENTS:

1 c. Spaghetti squash, cooked, buttered, seasoned

¼ c. Bacon, cooked, crumbled

1 Egg, poached

1 T. Green onions, chopped

Salt

Pepper

Layer spaghetti squash, egg, bacon and green onions.

Salt and pepper to taste.

scotch eggs

INGREDIENTS:

8 Eggs
1 lb. Ground sausage
¼ c. Parmesan cheese, grated
¼ c. Coconut flour
Salt
Pepper
¼ t. Garlic, minced
1 egg, beaten
Coconut oil for frying

Boil 7 eggs for 4 minutes: let eggs sit in hot water for five minutes. Remove eggs from pan and place in ice water.

In a mixing bowl, stir together sausage, coconut flour, Parmesan cheese, garlic, salt and pepper. Set aside.

Peel eggs and dry them. They need to be dry so that the sausage will stick to them.

Divide sausage into 7 equal portions, press into patties. Roll each patty around an egg.

Whisk remaining egg. Dip each sausage ball into egg then into Parmesan. Brown Scotch egg in hot oil on all sides.

spaghetti squash breakfast bake

INGREDIENTS:
4 c. Spaghetti squash "noodles"
1 T. Olive oil
1 t. Garlic, minced
1 lb. Pork sausage
1 c. Mushrooms, diced
1 c. Spinach, chopped
1 c. Feta cheese, crumbled
6 Eggs, beaten
¼ t. Salt
¼ t. Pepper
1 c. Grape tomatoes, quartered

Preheat oven to 400 degrees. Butter a 9x13-inch baking dish.
Set aside.

In a large pan, heat oil. Add garlic and sausage, cook until sausage crumbles.

Add mushrooms, spinach, feta, eggs, salt and pepper.

Bake for 45 minutes. Top with tomatoes.

sweet potato crusted quiche

INGREDIENTS:

2 Large sweet potatoes, grated
2 T. Coconut oil
9 Eggs
¼ t. Salt
¼ t. Pepper
¼ c. Almond milk
½ c. Tomatoes, diced
6 Strips bacon, cooked, crumbled
1 c. Spinach, chopped
1 T. Basil, chopped
1 T. Oregano
½ T. Chives
¼ c. Feta cheese

Preheat oven to 400 degrees.

Grease a 9-inch glass pie plate.

In a large bowl, mix the sweet potatoes, coconut oil, 1 egg and salt and pepper; mix well. Press into pie plate.

Bake for 30 minutes and slightly golden brown.

In a medium mixing bowl, whisk the remaining 8 eggs, salt, pepper and almond milk. Add tomatoes, bacon, spinach, herbs and feta cheese; mix well. Pour into pie crust.

Bake for 40 minutes or until egg is set and firm.

Remove from oven and let sit for 30 minutes.

eggs & sweet potato hash

INGREDIENTS:
½ c. Onion, chopped
3 T. Olive oil
1 t. Garlic, minced
2 Italian sausages, cooked, diced
2 Sweet potatoes, peeled, diced
3 T. Fresh rosemary, chopped
Salt and pepper
3 Eggs

In a large pan, heat oil.

Add onion and garlic, cook until golden brown.

Add sweet potatoes, sausage, rosemary, salt and pepper.

Cook until sweet potatoes are tender.

Crack eggs on hash, cover and let eggs cook until set.

salads

autumn salad

INGREDIENTS:

3 c. Salad greens

1 c. Butternut squash, diced, roasted

2 Chicken breasts, grilled, diced

½ Avocado, diced

¼ c. Almonds, sliced, toasted

2 Eggs, boiled, chopped

½ c. Beets, roasted, diced

¼ c. Cranberries, dried

Balsamic Vinaigrette Dressing

To roast the butternut squash and beets: dice the vegetables.

Put them in a large Ziploc bag with olive oil, salt and pepper and shake to coat.

Bake in the oven at 400 degrees until the vegetables are tender.

Let the vegetables cool.

Assemble all salad ingredients and top with balsamic vinaigrette.

avocado tomato salad

INGREDIENTS:
2 medium Tomatoes, diced
1 Avocado, diced
1 T. Olive oil
1 t. Italian seasoning
½ t. Garlic, minced
¼ c. Parmesan cheese
Salt
Pepper

Mix all ingredients.

Add salt and pepper to taste.

broccoli salad

INGREDIENTS:
¼ c. Red onion, chopped
2 T. Apple cider vinegar
½ c. Mayonnaise
1 Head broccoli, cut into florets
8 Strips bacon, cooked, crumbled
½ c. Golden raisins
¼ c. Walnuts, chopped
Salt and pepper to taste
1 c. Grapes, sliced
1 T. Honey

In a large bowl, add broccoli, onion, bacon, raisins, walnuts and grapes.

In a small bowl, mix apple cider vinegar, mayonnaise, salt and pepper and honey.

Add to salad and mix well.

chicken salad

INGREDIENTS:
2 ½ c. Chicken, cooked, diced
¼ c. Almonds, sliced
2 Stalks celery, diced
1 Apple, cored, diced
¼ c. Golden raisins
¼ c. Dried cranberries
1 t. Curry powder
¼ t. Cumin
Salt Pepper
4 c. Salad greens
1 c. Mayonnaise

In a medium bowl, mix all ingredients except the greens.
Mix well.

On a salad plate, place one cup of salad greens.

Top with a scoop of chicken salad.

cobb salad

INGREDIENTS:

3 c. Salad greens
1 c. Carrots, matchstick
1 c. Turkey breast, diced
1 Egg, hardboiled, diced
½ c. Bacon, crooked, crumbled
½ c. Cheese, grated

Assemble all ingredients; top with your favorite dressing.

egg salad

INGREDIENTS:

5 Eggs, Boiled, peeled, diced
¼ c. Bacon, cooked, crumbled
1 T. Chives
¼ t. Paprika
½ t. Garlic, minced
1 t. Honey
1 T. Golden mustard
¾ c. Mayonnaise
1 Stalk celery, chopped
Salt
Pepper
2 Tomatoes, sliced
4 c. Salad greens

In a medium bowl, combine eggs, bacon, chives, paprika, garlic, honey, mustard, mayo, celery, salt and pepper. Mix well.

On a salad plate, place one cup of salad greens, lay sliced tomatoes on top of greens.

Top with egg salad.

golden raisin pistachio salad

INGREDIENTS:
3 c. Salad greens
½ c. Gruyere cheese, grated
¼ c. Golden Raisins
¼ c. Pistachios

Mix all salad ingredients.

Top with Apple Cider Vinaigrette.

pea and parmesan salad

INGREDIENTS:
4 c. Snap peas, chopped
2 c. Chicken stock
1 T. Butter
1 c. Parmesan cheese, crumbled
Salt
Pepper

In a small pan, cook snap peas in chicken stock, just until tender. Drain.

Add butter, Parmesan cheese, salt and pepper.

Serve warm or cold.

pomegranate pear salad

INGREDIENTS:

3 c. Salad greens
1 Pear, peeled, sliced
¼ c. Pomegranate seeds
½ c. Walnuts, chopped
½ c. Dried cranberries
¼ c. Goat cheese crumbles
Balsamic Vinaigrette

Mix all salad ingredients.

Top with balsamic vinaigrette.

artichoke walnut spinach salad

INGREDIENTS:

4 c. Baby spinach

½ c. Beets, canned, matchstick, drained

¼ c. Cherries, dried

¼ c. Golden raisins, dried

½ c. Artichoke hearts, drained

¼ c. Walnuts, chopped

Balsamic Vinaigrette salad dressing

Mix all salad ingredients in a medium bowl, top with Balsamic vinaigrette.

spinach salad

INGREDIENTS:
2 Handfuls of fresh spinach
2 Eggs, boiled, finely diced
4 Strips Bacon, cooked, crumbled
6 Strawberries, sliced
½ c. Sliced almonds
½ c. Cranberries, dried

Mix all ingredients.

This salad is great with chicken or shrimp.

Serve with Raspberry vinaigrette.

watermelon feta salad

INGREDIENTS:
2 c. Salad greens
1 c. Watermelon, diced
½ c. Avocado, diced
¼ c. Almonds, sliced
¼ c. Feta, crumbled
Raspberry Vinaigrette

In a medium bowl, combine all ingredients.

asian meatball soup

INGREDIENTS:

1 t. Onion, dried
1 lb. Ground turkey
1 egg
1/3 c. Almond flour
1 t. Ginger,
1 T. Chives
1 T. Soy sauce or Coconut Aminos
1 t. Garlic, minced
Salt
2 c. Napa cabbage, chopped
2 c. Carrots, matchstick
½ c. Scallions
¼ c. Fresh cilantro
½ t. Lemon juice
1 t. Sesame oil
½ T Ginger, minced
½ T. Garlic, minced
6 c. Chicken broth
2 T. Soy sauce or Coconut Aminos
1 T. Fish sauce
Dash Red pepper flakes

Meatballs: Preheat oven to 400.

In a large bowl, combine onion, turkey, egg, flour, ginger, chives, soy sauce, garlic and salt. Mix well.

Using a small scoop, scoop out meatball mixture and roll into balls.

Bake meatballs on a baking sheet for 20 minutes, or until cooked through.

Soup: In a large soup pot, add all remaining ingredients as well
as the meatballs.

Simmer until heated through and vegetables are tender.

asian turkey soup

INGREDIENTS:

1 T. Coconut oil
2 t. Garlic, minced
1 T. Onion, dried
1 ½ lbs. Ground turkey
2 t. Ginger, minced
3 t. Five spice powder
1 ½ c. Broccoli, chopped
1 ½ c. Carrots, matchstick
1 c. Mushrooms, diced
3 c. Bean sprouts
2-32 oz. Chicken stock
1/8 c. Sweet chili sauce
¼ c. Cilantro, chopped
3 T. Hoisin sauce
¼ c. Soy sauce or Coconut Aminos

In a soup pan, heat oil.

Add onion, garlic, turkey, ginger and five spice powder.

Cook until turkey is no longer pink, drain.

Add all other ingredients. Bring to a boil.

Then lower the temperature and simmer for 30 minutes.

beef stew

INGREDIENTS:

2 lbs. Stew meat, chopped
1 T. Olive oil
1 T. Onion, dried
1 t. Garlic, minced
2 Large carrots, diced
2 Sweet potatoes, diced
2 Stalks celery, diced
½ t. Rosemary
½ t. Parsley
1 c. Crushed tomatoes
2 T. Dijon mustard
2 c. Beef broth
¼ c. Wine vinegar
2 T. Arrowroot powder
Salt
Pepper

In a large soup pot, heat olive oil.

Add beef, onion, garlic, rosemary and parsley. Cook until meat is browned on all sides.

Add carrots, sweet potatoes and celery.

Cook until vegetables are tender.

Add arrowroot powder; mix well.

Add crushed tomatoes, mustard, wine vinegar and beef broth. Season with salt and pepper.

Simmer until heated through.

broccoli cheddar soup

INGREDIENTS:

2 ½ c. Broccoli florets
1 c. Carrots, matchstick
4 c. Chicken broth
½ t. Garlic powder
½ c. Bacon, cooked, crumbled
2 c. Cheddar cheese
1 can Coconut milk
½ T. Onion, dried
1 T. Arrowroot powder
1 T. Water

In a large soup pot, add broccoli, carrots, broth, garlic, bacon, cheese, coconut milk and onion.

Cook until vegetables are tender.

Mix arrowroot powder and water.

Add to soup; cook until soup thickens.

cauliflower chowder

INGREDIENTS:
½ c. Bacon, cooked, crumbled
3 T. Butter
½ T. Garlic powder
1 T. Onion, dried
1 c. Carrots, matchstick
2 Stalks celery, chopped
1 Head cauliflower, chopped
¼ c. Almond flour
4 c. Chicken broth
1 c. Almond milk
Salt
Pepper
1 t. Parsley
1 t. Chives

In a large soup pot, melt butter; add garlic, onion, carrots, celery and cauliflower. Cook until vegetables are tender.

Add almond flour and mix well.

Add bacon, broth, milk, salt, pepper, parsley and chives.

chipotle chicken tomato soup

INGREDIENTS:

4 c. Chicken, cooked, diced
1 29 oz. can Petite diced tomatoes
1 15 oz. can Tomato sauce
1 c. Coconut milk
1 T. Cilantro, dried
1 pkg. Taco seasoning
1 T. Garlic, minced
1 T. Onion, dried

In a large soup pot, add all ingredients and cook 20 minutes.

coconut curry soup

INGREDIENTS:

1 T. Coconut oil
1 lb. Ground turkey
1 t. Garlic, minced
¼ t. Basil, dried
¼ t. Lime juice
2 T. Curry powder
½ t. Cilantro, dried
½ t. Ginger, minced
1 c. Mushrooms, sliced
1 ½ c. Carrots, matchstick
1 Zucchini, spiraled
32 oz. Chicken stock
1-14 oz. can Coconut milk

In a large soup pot, heat coconut oil.

Add ground turkey, garlic, basil, lime juice, curry, cilantro and ginger. Cook until turkey is cooked through. Drain.

Add mushrooms, carrots and zucchini, cook 5 minutes.

Add chicken stock and coconut milk.

Salt and pepper to taste.

grilled butternut and bacon soup

INGREDIENTS:

1 Butternut squash, diced
8 Strips bacon, chopped
1 T. Garlic, minced
Salt and pepper
1 T. Olive oil
½ t. Thyme
½ t. Rosemary
½ t. Cumin
2½ c. Chicken stock
¼ c. Goat cheese, crumbled
2 t. Chives

Preheat oven to 400 degrees. Line baking sheet with parchment paper.

In a large bowl, add bacon, butternut squash, salt, pepper and olive oil, stir. Arrange butternut squash in a single layer on the baking sheet. Roast butternut squash for 25-30 minutes, or until butternut squash is tender.

Meanwhile, cook, drain and crumble remaining bacon. Set aside.

In a large soup pot, add roasted butternut squash, thyme, rosemary, cumin and chicken stock, heat through.

Put soup in a blender and pulse until soup is smooth. Pour soup into bowls and top with bacon, goat cheese and chives.

sausage vegetable soup

INGREDIENTS:

1 Lb. Pork sausage

1 T. Onion, dried

1 T. Garlic, minced

1 t. Oregano

1 t. Basil

¼ c. Sundried tomatoes, chopped

4 Stalks celery, diced

1 ½ c. Carrots, matchstick

1 small Zucchini, diced

1 small Yellow squash, diced

1 - 28oz. can Petite diced tomatoes

3 T. Tomato paste

2 - 15oz. cans Chicken stock

Salt and pepper to taste

In a large pan, brown sausage. Drain, reserving 1 T. of fat, and set aside.

In the same large pan with 1 T. of the sausage fat, add onion, garlic, celery oregano and basil.

Sauté until vegetables are tender.

In a large soup pot, add sausage, sautéed vegetables, sundried tomatoes, carrots, zucchini, yellow squash, canned tomatoes, tomato paste and chicken stock. Cook until all vegetables are tender.

Add salt and pepper if needed.

sausage, sweet potato & kale soup

INGREDIENTS:

2 Large sweet potatoes, peeled, diced

1 lb. Spicy sausage

1 T. Onion, dried

1 T. Garlic, minced

1 bunch Kale, chopped

6 c. Chicken stock

½ c. Coconut milk

Salt

Pepper

Dash Red pepper flakes

In a large soup pot, add sausage, onion and garlic.

Cook until meat is cooked through and no longer pink. Drain.

Add all other ingredients and cook until vegetables are tender.

scallops in vegetable ragout

INGREDIENTS:
1 lb. Scallops
2 T. Butter, divided
Salt
Pepper
1 c. Carrots, sliced
1 T. Onions, dried
2 Stalks celery, diced
1 medium Sweet potato, diced
1 t. Garlic, minced
½ t. Thyme
½ t. Rosemary
1 c. Crushed tomatoes
1 c. Chicken broth

In a soup pot, melt 1 T. butter.

Add onion, garlic, carrots, celery and sweet potato. Cook until vegetables are tender.

Add garlic, thyme, rosemary, tomatoes and broth. Simmer 15 minutes.

Meanwhile, heat 1 T. butter in pan.

Add scallops; season with salt and pepper. Cook for 3-5 minutes on each side. Be careful not to overcook scallops or they can become rubbery.

In a soup bowl, ladle a scoop of ragout and top with scallops.

sweet potato chili

INGREDIENTS:

1 T. Olive oil
2 lbs. Ground beef
1 T. Onion, dried
½ t. Garlic, minced
2-28 oz. Crushed tomatoes
3 c. Chicken stock
1 c. Carrots, matchstick
2 Large sweet potatoes, diced
1 t. Thyme
½ t. Salt
½ t. Pepper
1 ½ t. Chili powder
Dash Oregano
Dash Red pepper flakes

In a large soup pot, heat olive oil.

Add beef, onion and garlic. Cook until beef is cooked through. Drain.

Add all other ingredients and simmer until vegetables are tender.

thai coconut soup

INGREDIENTS:
3 c. Chicken, cooked, diced
1 T. Coconut oil
1 c. Coconut cream, unsweetened
1-32oz carton Chicken broth
1 C. Carrots, diced
3 Stalks celery, chopped
2 c. Sweet potatoes, chopped
1 ½ T. Curry powder
1 t. Ginger, minced
1 T. Garlic, minced
1 T. Cilantro

Put all ingredients into a large soup pot.

Cook until vegetables are tender.

Salt and pepper to taste.

tomato basil soup

INGREDIENTS:
¼ c. Onion, diced
3 T. Olive oil
1 T. Basil, dried
1 t. Oregano
1-15 oz. can Tomato sauce
1-28 oz. can Crushed tomatoes
2 c. Chicken stock
1 t. Salt
1 c. Coconut milk
1 t. Parsley
Salt
Pepper

In a soup pan, heat olive oil.

Add onion, cook until brown and tender.

Add all other ingredients.

Cook for 30 minutes.

dressings
& condiments

baconnaise

INGREDIENTS:
3 Egg yolks
1 ½ T. Lemon juice
1 t. Dijon mustard
1 c. Bacon fat, cooled
Sat and pepper to taste

In a small blender, mix together the egg yolks, lemon juice and mustard about 30 seconds.

Add ¼ cup of the bacon fat and blend again.

Slowly add the rest of the bacon fat while blending.

Add salt and pepper to taste.

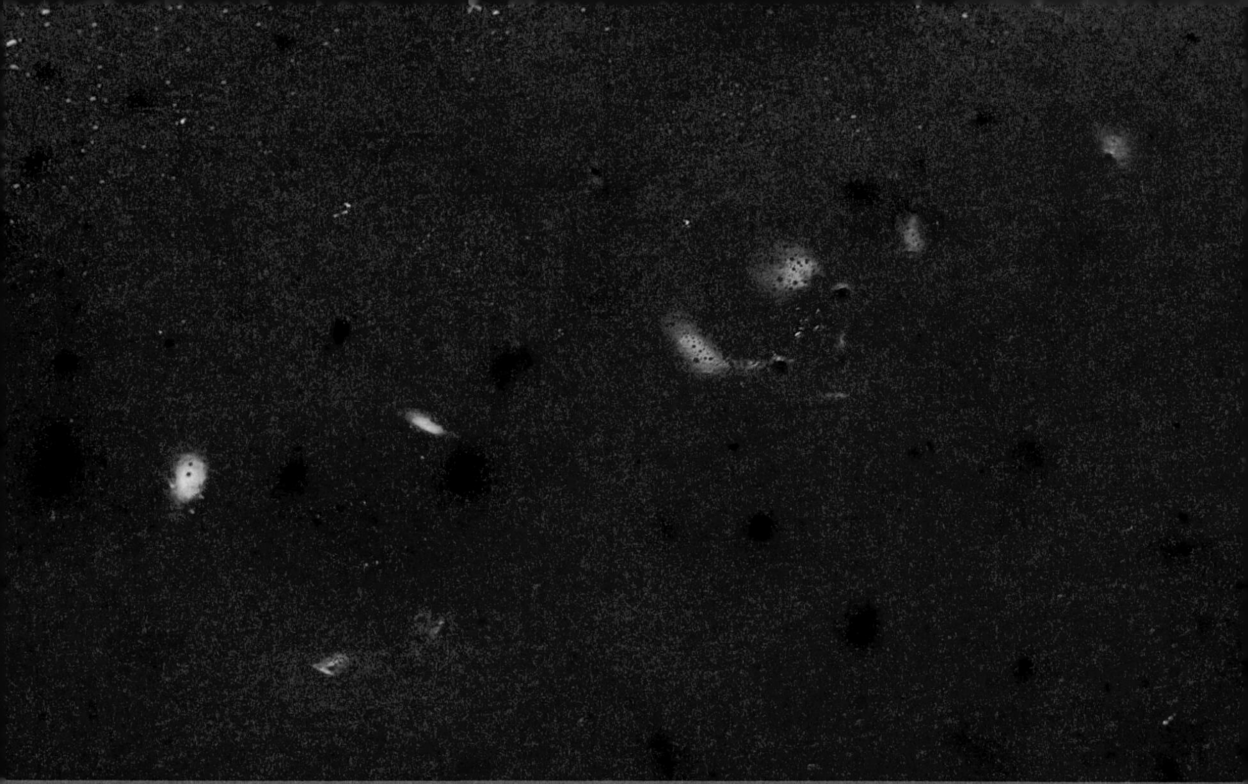

balsamic vinaigrette

INGREDIENTS:

1 c. Balsamic vinegar
1 c. Olive oil
1 t. Oregano
1 t. Garlic, minced
Salt and Pepper to taste

Combine all ingredients and mix well.

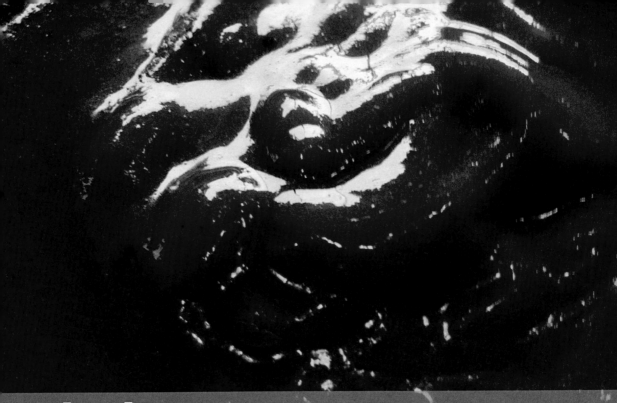

barbeque sauce

INGREDIENTS:

1 t. Coconut oil
1 T. Onion, chopped
1 T. Garlic, minced
1 c. Tomato paste
1 t. Liquid smoke
½ c. Apple cider vinegar
½ c. Water
1 T. Worcestershire sauce
¼ c. Ketchup
3 T. Mustard
¼ t. Cloves
¼ t. Cinnamon
2 dashes Tabasco

Heat oil in a saucepan, add onion and garlic.

Cook until onion is browned.

Add all other ingredients. Simmer for 30 minutes.

Put sauce in a blender, and blend until smooth.

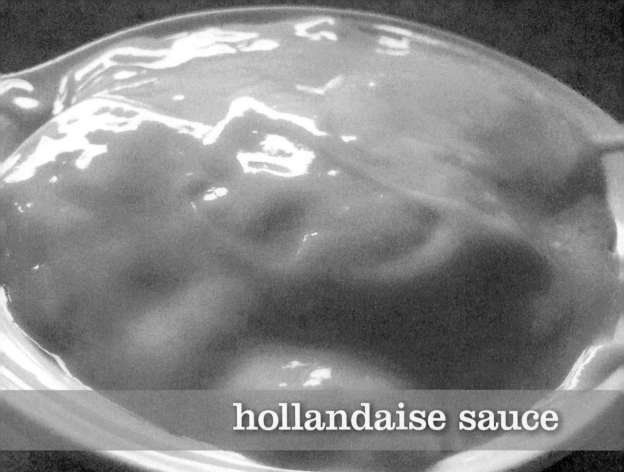

hollandaise sauce

INGREDIENTS:
3 T. Coconut oil, melted, cooled
2 Egg yolks
1 T. Lemon juice
½ t. Salt
⅛ t. Paprika

Fill a blender with boiling water and let sit for 10 minutes.

Pour water out and dry completely.

Pour in eggs, and seasonings; blend well.

Slowly blend in coconut oil and blend until smooth.

honey mustard dressing

INGREDIENTS:
⅓ c. Mayonnaise
1 T. Garlic, minced
2 T. Golden mustard
2 T. Honey
¼ t. Cayenne

In a blender, add all ingredients. Mix well.

ketchup

INGREDIENTS:

1 c. Tomato paste
⅔ c. Apple cider vinegar
⅓ c. Water
2 T. Honey
2 T. Onion, diced
1 T. Garlic, minced
1 t. Salt
⅛ t. Allspice
⅛ t. Cloves
⅛ t. Pepper

In a blender, mix all ingredients until smooth.

marinara sauce

INGREDIENTS:
1 T. Olive oil
1 T. Garlic, minced
1 T. Onion, dried
½ t. Oregano
½ t. Basil
Salt
Pepper
2 lbs. Roma tomatoes, chopped

In saucepan, heat oil. Add onion and garlic.

Cook until onions are golden brown.

Add all other ingredients and simmer for 30 minutes.

mayonaise

INGREDIENTS:

2 Eggs
1 T. Lemon juice
1 T. White wine vinegar
1 t. Dry mustard
2 dashes Tabasco sauce
¼ t. Salt
1 c. Olive oil

Using a small blender, like a smoothie blender, combine eggs, lemon juice, white wine vinegar, mustard, tabasco, salt.

Blend well. With the blender running, slowly add the olive oil.

parmesan ranch dressing

INGREDIENTS:

½ c. Mayonnaise

½ c. Almond milk

1 T. Chives

1 T. Parsley

1 T. Red onion, minced

¼ t. Garlic, minced

¼ t. Paprika

Salt and pepper to taste

¼ c. Parmesan cheese, finely grated

Whisk together all ingredients until well combined.

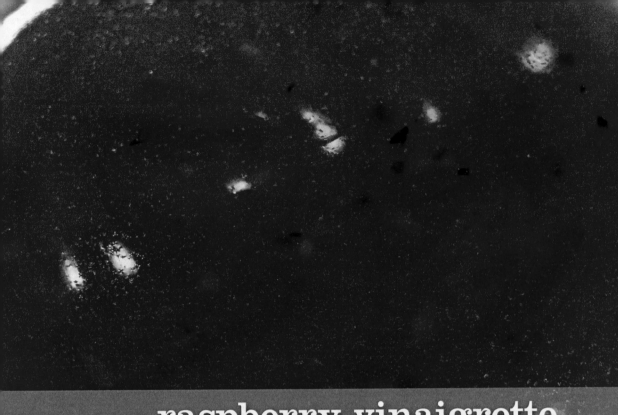

raspberry vinaigrette

INGREDIENTS:
½ c. Fresh raspberries
2 T. Lemon juice
2 T. Red wine vinegar
1 t. Honey
Pinch of salt
¼ c. Olive oil

Whisk together all ingredients until mixed well.

sweet chili sauce

INGREDIENTS:

4 Red Chili Peppers
1 T. Garlic, minced
½ c. White wine vinegar
1 c. Honey
1 ½ c. Water
1 t. Salt
4 ½ t. Arrowroot powder
4 ½ t. Water
1 t. Ginger, minced

In a medium saucepan, add all ingredients except the arrowroot powder and 4 ½ t. water.

Cook until boiling.

Whisk together water and arrowroot powder.

Add to the sauce and blend well.

Cook until thickened.

teriyaki sauce

INGREDIENTS:

½ c. Soy sauce
  or Coconut aminos
½ c. Honey
¼ c. Orange juice
2 T. Rice vinegar
1 T. Ginger, minced
1 T. Garlic, minced
1 T. Sesame oil
⅛ t. Red pepper flakes
¼ t. Sesame seeds
1 t. Water
1 t. Arrowroot powder

In a saucepan, mix soy sauce, honey, orange juice, rice vinegar, garlic, ginger, sesame oil, red pepper flakes.

Cook for 5 minutes.

Whisk together water and arrowroot powder.

Add to teriyaki sauce.

Simmer until sauce starts to thicken.

Sprinkle in sesame seeds.

main dishes

asian beef lettuce cups

INGREDIENTS:

1 lb. Ground beef
½ c. Onion, chopped
1 c. Mushrooms, sliced
2 T. Butter
1 T. Garlic, minced
2 c. Broccoli slaw
½ c. Carrots, matchstick
2 Scallions, sliced
¼ c. Cilantro, chopped
1 t. Fish sauce
1 T. Apple cider vinegar
2 T. Soy sauce
Salt
Pepper
1 T. Ginger, minced
1 t. Red pepper flakes
¼ c. Sweet chili sauce
Butter lettuce

Brown ground beef. Drain.

In a large pan, melt butter. Add mushroom, onion, garlic, broccoli slaw and carrots. Cook until vegetables are tender.

Add scallions, cilantro, fish sauce, apple cider vinegar, soy sauce, salt and pepper, ginger, red pepper flakes and sweet chili sauce. Add in beef. Cook until heated through.

Serve on butter lettuce leaves.

ginger orange scallops

INGREDIENTS:
4 T. Coconut oil
2 lbs. Large scallops
Salt and Pepper
2 t. Garlic, minced
¼ c. Soy sauce
  or Coconut Aminos
¼ T. Orange juice
2 T. Water
2 T. Butter
½ t. Ginger, minced

Lay the scallops on a paper towel and dry them well. Sprinkle both sides with salt and pepper. Set aside.

Heat oil in large sauté pan; add scallops, making sure not to crowd them.

You may need to cook them in batches.

Meanwhile, mix soy sauce or coconut aminos, orange juice, water, butter and ginger. Set aside.

After removing the scallops from the pan, add liquid mixture, making sure to get all the scallop drippings off the bottom of the pan.

Reduce the heat and cook 2-3 minutes. Spoon sauce over the scallops.

baked tilapia with lemon

INGREDIENTS:

4 Tilapia filets
3 T. Lemon juice
1 T. Butter, melted
1 t. Garlic, minced
½ c. Tomatoes, diced
1 t. Parsley flakes
Pepper to taste

Preheat oven to 375 degrees. Spray a baking dish with non-stick cooking spray.

Rinse tilapia filets under cool water, and pat dry with paper towels.

Place filets in baking dish. Drizzle lemon juice and butter over tilapia. Sprinkle with garlic, tomatoes, parsley, and pepper.

Bake for 30 minutes, or until the fish is no longer translucent and flakes when pulled apart with a fork.

balsamic maple salmon

INGREDIENTS:
4 Salmon filets
2 T. Maple syrup
2 T. Balsamic vinaigrette
2 t. Garlic, minced
2 t. Olive oil
Salt
Pepper
1 t. Butter

In a small bowl, combine maple syrup, balsamic vinaigrette, garlic, olive oil, salt and pepper. Mix well.

Pour half of the mixture into a large Ziploc bag, add salmon. Marinate salmon for half hour.

Preheat oven to 375 degrees. Spread a baking sheet with butter. Lay salmon on baking sheet and bake for 15 minutes, turning once.

Meanwhile, heat remaining sauce. Pour sauce over salmon filets and bake an additional five minutes.

balsamic rosemary flank steak

INGREDIENTS:
1 ½ lbs. Flank steak
1 t. Garlic, minced
½ t. Rosemary, dried
¼ c. Balsamic vinegar
Salt
Pepper
¼ c. Olive oil
½ c. Dry red wine

Put all ingredients into a large Ziploc bag and mix well.

Marinate steak for 1 hour, up to overnight.

Grill steak for 6-10 minutes per side, depending on how well you like your meat cooked.

Let the steak sit for 5-10 before slicing.

bbq turkey breast

INGREDIENTS:

1 ½ lbs. Turkey breast
1 t. Butter
1 t. Garlic, minced
¼ t. Salt
¼ t. Pepper
1 t. Olive oil
2 T. BBQ sauce
1 c. Chicken broth

Preheat oven to 350 degrees.

Lightly butter an 8x8-baking dish.

In a small bowl, mix salt, pepper, garlic, and oil. Rub mixture on all sides of turkey breasts. Rub on bbq sauce.

Put turkey in baking dish.

Pour chicken broth into baking dish, being careful to not pour over turkey.

Bake for 35-40 minutes, or until juices run clear. Remove from oven. Let stand for 10 minutes before slicing.

beef and broccoli

INGREDIENTS:

1 lb. Beef strips
2 c. Broccoli florets
1 T. Arrowroot powder
1 T. Coconut oil
1 t. Garlic, minced
1 t. Ginger, minced
½ c. Sweet chili sauce
½ c. Hoisin sauce
1 t. Sesame oil

In a large pan, melt coconut oil. Add garlic and ginger.

In a medium bowl, mix the beef with the arrowroot powder.

Add to the pan, cook for five minutes.

Add broccoli, sweet chili sauce, hoisin sauce and sesame oil.

Cook until broccoli is tender.

berry glazed crockpot chicken

INGREDIENTS:
4 Chicken breasts
4 medium Sweet potatoes
Sesame seeds
Glaze:
½ c. Honey
½ c. Soy sauce
2 T. Olive oil
½ c. Blackberry jam
2 t. Butter
1 t. Apple cider vinegar
½ t. Sesame seeds
1 T. Garlic, minced
¼ t. Crushed red pepper flakes

In a small bowl, mix all glaze ingredients. Set aside.

Put chicken in crockpot and pour glaze over chicken.

Cook on high for three hours, turn chicken and cook another hour.

Meanwhile, bake sweet potatoes.

Remove chicken and shred with a fork.

Put sauce into a saucepan and heat to boil, reduce heat and simmer until sauce thickens. Add chicken to sauce.

Top each sweet potato with chicken, top with sesame seeds.

spaghetti squash bolognese sauce

INGREDIENTS:

2 T. Coconut oil
1 ½ lbs. Ground turkey
1 ½ lbs. Ground pork
¼ t. Salt
¼ t. Pepper
1 c. Mushrooms, diced
1½ c. Matchstick carrots
½ c. Celery, diced
1 Onion, diced
1 t. Garlic, minced
1 t. Oregano
1 t. Marjoram
1 t. Basil
½ t. Cinnamon
1 - 15 oz. can Petite diced
tomatoes
1 - 28 oz. can Crushed tomatoes
1 Large Spaghetti squash
2 t. Butter

Preheat oven to 400 degrees. Cut spaghetti squash in half lengthwise. Scoop out seeds and pulp. Poke spaghetti squash with fork repeatedly. Place spaghetti squash cut side down onto baking dish. Bake for 40 minutes or until squash is tender.

In a large sauté pan, add coconut oil, onion, garlic, vegetables; sauté until vegetables are tender. Add meats and seasonings: cook until meat is no longer pink.

Add tomatoes and cook until it starts to boil. Reduce heat and simmer 20 minutes.

Serve meat sauce over spaghetti squash.

braised lamb shank

INGREDIENTS:

3 T. Olive oil
2-3 Lamb shanks
Salt and pepper
2 T. Garlic, minced
1 Sweet onion, diced
⅓ c. Chicken stock
1 T. Dijon mustard
2 T. Balsamic vinegar
2 t. Soy sauce
2 sprigs Fresh rosemary

Preheat oven to 400 degrees. Season lamb shanks with salt and pepper.

In a large pan, heat 2 T. olive oil. Brown lamb shanks on all sides; place lamb shanks in a Dutch oven.

In the same large pan, heat the remaining oil. Add the garlic and onions and cook until golden brown.

Pour in chicken stock and loosen any drippings from lamb shanks, add dijon, balsamic vinegar, and soy sauce.

Pour the sauce over the lamb shanks, add rosemary sprigs.

Bake for 2 hours or until meat is very tender.

butter & herb baked tilapia

INGREDIENTS:

4 Tilapia filets
2 T. Butter, melted
1 t. Lemon juice
½ t. Golden mustard
¼ t. Parsley
¼ t. Dill
1 t. Garlic, minced
Salt and pepper

Preheat oven to 375 degrees.

Line a large baking dish with parchment paper.

Put fish on lined baking dish

Whisk together all other ingredients.

Top the fish with the sauce.

Bake for 15-16 minutes, then broil for 1-2 minutes or until fish is golden brown.

butter lemon cod

INGREDIENTS:
4 Cod filets
¼ c. Butter, melted
2 T. Lemon juice
¼ c. Almond flour
¼ t. Paprika
¼ t. Parsley
Salt
Pepper
1 T. Olive oil

In a small bowl, combine lemon juice and butter. Set aside.

In another small bowl, combine almond flour, paprika, parsley, salt and pepper.

In a frying pan, heat oil. Dip cod filet in the lemon butter mixture and then into the flour mixture, coating each side well.

Cook on each side for 5 minutes, or until done to your likeness.

chicken parmesan

INGREDIENTS:

4 Chicken breasts
2 T. Olive oil
1 T. Dried onion
1 t. Garlic, minced
Salt
Pepper
½ t. Oregano
½ t. Basil
2 T. Tomato paste
1 - 28 oz. can Petite diced tomatoes
1 c. Mozzarella cheese, grated
Parsley flakes

Preheat oven to 350 degrees.

In a large pan, heat 1 T. olive oil.

Season chicken with salt and pepper on each side. Cook chicken for 4 minutes on each side. Place chicken in a 9x13 baking dish.

In the pan, add 1 T. Olive oil. Add onion, garlic, salt, pepper, oregano, and basil. Cook until onions are tender.

Add tomato paste and diced tomatoes. Simmer for 10 minutes.

Pour tomato sauce over chicken and top with mozzarella cheese. Sprinkle with parsley. Bake for 30 minutes.

chicken saltimbocca

INGREDIENTS:

1 T. Olive oil
1 t. Garlic, minced
1 T. Onion, dried
2 Chicken breasts, cut into strips
½ t. Sage
4 Slices prosciutto
1 c. Chicken broth
1 T. Arrowroot powder

Mix sage, dried onion and garlic and set aside.

Lay a strip of prosciutto, then place a chicken strip onto prosciutto, put sage mixture onto each piece of chicken. Roll up chicken and secure with a toothpick.

Heat oil. Cook chicken until no longer pink inside. Remove the chicken from the pan and set aside.

Pour chicken broth into pan and bring to a boil and loosen any dripping from the chicken.

Mix arrowroot powder with 1 T. water.

Add to the chicken broth and stir until sauce thickens. Pour over chicken.

apricot mustard chicken

INGREDIENTS:

4 Chicken breasts
1 t. Olive oil
½ t. Cayenne pepper
1 T. Thyme
1 ½ t. Pepper
1 t. Garlic, minced
Salt
½ c. Apricot jam
2 T. Brown mustard

In a large Ziploc, combine cayenne pepper, thyme, pepper, salt and garlic.

Add chicken breasts and shake until chicken is well coated. Refrigerate for at least 10 minutes.

Meanwhile, in a small pan, mix apricots jam and mustard; cook until well blended and heated through.

Grill chicken for 4 minutes on both sides.

Top with apricot and mustard sauce.

goat cheese pomegranate chicken

INGREDIENTS:
4 Chicken breasts
1 T. Olive oil
1 c. Balsamic vinegrette
½ c. Goat cheese, crumbled
½ c. Pomegranate Arils
¼ c. Fresh basil, chopped

Marinate chicken in balsamic vinaigrette for at least 30 minutes.

In a large pan, heat olive oil.

Cook chicken for 6 minutes each side, or until chicken is no longer pink.

Top chicken breast with goat cheese, pomegranate arils and basil.

peach chutney chicken

INGREDIENTS:

4 Chicken breasts, cut into strips
1 T. Olive oil
¼ t. Cumin
¼ t. Cinnamon
Salt
Pepper
Peach Chutney:
1-½ lbs. Peaches, peeled, pitted, diced
1 T. Olive oil
½ c. Onion, diced
2 t. Garlic, minced
¼ t. Red pepper flakes
1 c. Apple cider vinegar
¼ c. Honey
½ c Raisins
Salt and pepper

Heat oil; add onion and garlic and sauté until soft, ten minutes.

Add red pepper flakes and stir one minute, until fragrant.

Add peaches, vinegar, honey, and raisins, and season with salt and pepper. Bring to boil, reduce heat and continue cooking on medium low until peaches soften, about twenty minutes. Add water if the liquid boils out before the peaches have fully cooked.

Heat olive oil in pan. Season chicken breasts on both sides.

Cook chicken for 5 minutes per side, or until chicken is no longer pink. Top with peach chutney.

asparagus mushroom stir fry

INGREDIENTS:

1½ lbs Chicken breasts
½ c. Chicken stock
2 T. Soy sauce
   or Coconut aminos
2 T. Arrowroot powder
2 T. Water
1 T. Olive oil
1 Bunch asparagus, ends
trimmed and cut into 2" pieces
1 ½ c. Mushrooms, sliced
1 T. Garlic, minced
1 T. Ginger, fresh ground
3 T. Lemon juice
¼ t. Pepper

In a small bowl, combine chicken stock and soy sauce.

In another small bowl, combine water and arrowroot powder until smooth. In a small sauce pan, combine ingredients in both bowls and cook until sauce thickens, set aside.

In a large sauté pan, heat 1 T. Olive oil, then add asparagus and mushrooms.

Saute only until tender, remove from pan and set aside.

Add remaining olive oil to pan, along with garlic and chicken, sauté for 5 minutes.

Then add vegetables and sauce and cook until heated through.

peach sweet potato chicken skewers

INGREDIENTS:

1 Medium sweet potato, peeled and cut into cubes
1 c. White wine vinegar
½ c. + 1 T. Honey
2 T. Olive oil
Salt
Pepper
1 lb. Chicken breasts, cubed
2 Peaches, peeled and cut into chunks
½ c. Pecans, chopped
½ t. Cumin
½ t. Pumpkin pie spice

Soak skewers in water for 15 minutes

In a small saucepan, boil sweet potatoes until tender, but not soft. Drain. Set aside.

In another small saucepan, combine white wine vinegar, ½ c. honey, 1 T. oil, and salt and pepper. Simmer until sauce thickens.

Thread chicken, sweet potatoes and peaches onto skewers. Brush skewers with glaze. Grill until golden brown on all sides.

Meanwhile, in a small bowl, add pecans, 1 T. honey, 1 T. oil, cumin, pumpkin pie spice, salt and pepper. Cook the pecans until hot and glazed.

Remove skewers from grill, drizzle with glaze and sprinkle with pecans.

chicken curry

INGREDIENTS:
3 Lbs. Chicken breast, diced
2 T. Olive oil
1 T. Garlic, minced
¼ c. Onion, minced
1 T. Ginger
¼ c. Fresh cilantro, chopped
¼ c. Fresh basil, chopped
3 T. Curry powder
2 cans Coconut milk, full fat
1 T. Fish sauce
2 med. Sweet potatoes, diced
1 c. Cashews

Boil diced sweet potatoes until tender, drain and set aside.

In a large sauté pan, heat olive oil: add onion, ginger and garlic and sauté for 2 minutes.

Add chicken and cook for five minutes.

Add cilantro, basil, curry, coconut milk, fish sauce, sweet potatoes and cashews.

Cook until heated through and flavors are well blended.

chipotle chicken

INGREDIENTS:

4 Chicken breasts
2 Tomatoes, sliced
¼ c. Fresh cilantro, chopped
¼ t. Adobo seasoning
1 T. Lime juice
2 t. Honey
1 t. Garlic, minced
¼ t. Cumin
1 Large avocado, sliced

In a food processor, combine cilantro, lime juice, chipotle, honey, garlic, cumin and adobe. Mix well.

Put 1/2 of the sauce in a Ziploc bag and add chicken.

Marinade for 15 minutes. Remove chicken from marinade and grill chicken for 5 minutes on both sides.

Remove chicken from grill, top with sliced tomatoes, avocados and salsa.

cilantro thai chicken

INGREDIENTS:

¼ c. Olive oil
½ c. Fresh cilantro
2 T. Fish sauce
1 T. Sesame oil
1 t. Ginger, ground
1 t. Garlic, minced
2 T. Soy sauce
  or Coconut aminos
2 lbs. Chicken tenderloins
1 T. Sesame seeds

Put all ingredients in a large Ziploc bag.

Marinate chicken for one hour, up to overnight.

Grill chicken until chicken is no longer pink inside.

coconut pineapple meatballs

INGREDIENTS:

1 ½ c. Coconut, shredded

1 t. Salt, divided

1 t. Cayenne

1 c. Fresh pineapple, crushed, drained

2 T. Soy sauce
  or Coconut Aminos

1 t. Ginger, minced

1 t. Garlic, minced

2 Eggs, beaten

2 lbs. Ground pork

Preheat oven to 375 degrees.

In a small pan, add coconut, ¼ t. cayenne and ¼ t. salt. Cook until coconut starts to brown. Set aside.

In a medium bowl, add all other ingredients and mix well.

Using a small ice cream scoop, scoop meat mixture and roll into balls.

Roll meatballs into coconut mixture.

Put meatballs onto a baking sheet lined with parchment paper.

Bake meatballs for 20-30 minutes until sizzling and golden brown.

cranberry almond chicken

INGREDIENTS:

4 Boneless, skinless chicken breasts
2 Shallots, chopped
1 Leek, chopped
3 T. Butter
½ c. Cider vinegar
½ c. Maple syrup
¼ t. Ground nutmeg
½ c. Dried cranberries
1/3 c. Slivered almonds
Salt
Pepper

Preheat oven to 450 degrees.

Coat a baking dish with cooking spray.

Put chicken breasts in pan and season with salt and pepper.

In a small saucepan, combine vinegar, syrup, nutmeg, shallots and leeks: bring to a boil.

Reduce heat and cook until thickened and reduced by half.

In a small bowl, combine butter, cranberries and almonds.

Pour sauce over chicken and bake for 20 minutes. Sprinkle butter mixture over chicken and bake another 5-10 minutes.

crispy almond chicken

INGREDIENTS:

1 c. Olive oil
1 ¼ c. Almond flour
3 T. Arrowroot powder
½ t. Salt
½ t. Pepper
¼ c. Almond milk
2 Eggs, beaten
6 Chicken breasts, cut into strips

In a large pan, heat oil.

Preheat oven to 400 degrees.

In a shallow bowl, mix almond milk and egg to create an egg wash. In another small bowl, add almond flour, arrowroot powder, salt and pepper.

Dip each strip of chicken into egg wash, then into flour mixture.

Then put chicken into the oil and fry for one minute on each side.

Then put chicken onto a baking sheet and bake for 30 minutes, or until chicken in no longer pink inside.

cumin chicken tenders

INGREDIENTS:

4 Chicken breasts, cut into strips
1 T. Olive oil
Salt
Pepper
¼ t. Cumin
¼ t. Pumpkin pie spice

In a large Ziploc bag, add salt, pepper, cumin and pumpkin pie spice. Mix well.

Add chicken and shake until the chicken is well coated with spices.

Heat oil in a large pan, cook chicken until golden brown on each side. Do not over crowd pan.

dijon garlic salmon

INGREDIENTS:

2 Salmon filets
1 t. Garlic, minced
½ T. Olive oil
½ T. Dijon mustard
1 t. Lemon juice
1 t. Parsley
Salt
Pepper

Preheat oven to 375 degrees.

Spray a baking sheet with cooking spray.

In a small bowl combine garlic, olive oil, dijon mustard, lemon juice, parsley, salt and pepper. Mix well.

Coat salmon filets liberally with the Dijon mixture.

Put salmon filets onto the baking sheet and bake for 15 minutes, turning once.

garlic & paprika shrimp

INGREDIENTS:

1/3 c. Olive oil

12 Large shrimp, uncooked, deveined

1 t. Garlic, minced

1 t. Paprika

Salt and pepper to taste

Shell shrimp.

Combine all ingredients in a large Ziploc bag and let shrimp marinate for 30 minutes.

Cook shrimp until they are pink throughout.

ginger lime shrimp

INGREDIENTS:

1 ½ lbs. Shrimp, peeled, deveined

2 T. Lime juice

¼ t. Crushed red pepper flakes

1 T. Garlic, minced

2 t. Ginger, minced

¼ t. Salt

¼ t. Pepper

2 T. Cilantro, chopped

1 T. Olive oil

In a large Ziploc bag, mix all ingredients and let marinade for 30 minutes.

Grill shrimp 2-3 minutes per side.

grilled lamb chops & squash

INGREDIENTS:

1 T. Garlic, minced
½ c. Fresh parsley, chopped
4 T. Olive oil
1 ½ T. Shallots, chopped
1 t. Oregano
1 ½ t. Cooking sherry
1 ½ t. Lemon juice
¼ t. Crushed red pepper
1 t. Salt, divided
1 t. Pepper
3 Yellow squash, sliced
3 Zucchini, sliced
6 Lamb chops

Place garlic, parsley, 2 T. olive oil, shallots, oregano, cooking sherry, lemon juice, red pepper flakes in a food processor and process until smooth. Set aside.

Preheat oven to 450 degrees. Preheat grill to med-high heat.

Combine yellow squash, zucchini and 1 T. olive oil, salt and pepper: toss well. Arrange yellow squash and zucchini in a single layer on a baking sheet and bake for 16 minutes, turning once.

Lightly coat lamb chops with olive oil and season with salt and pepper.

Grill to your desired degree of doneness. Divide squash and zucchini among six plates, top each serving with 1 lamb chop.

peach avocado salsa skirt steak

INGREDIENTS:

3 lbs. Skirt steak
1 T. Garlic, minced
1 c. Fresh parsley, chopped
1 c. Fresh cilantro, chopped
1 t. Salt
2 T. Lemon juice
1 t. Pepper
1 t. Red pepper flakes
1 T. Olive oil
1 t. Chives

Peach and Avocado Salsa:
1 Peach, seeded, chopped
1 Avocado, seeded, chopped
½ t. Garlic, minced
½ c. Grape tomatoes, sliced
1 T. Red onion, diced
1 t. Lime juice
Salt
Pepper

In a large Ziploc bag, add garlic, parsley, cilantro, salt, lemon juice, pepper, red pepper flakes and olive oil. Mix well.

Add steak to Ziploc bag and let meat marinade for ½ hour.

Meanwhile, in a small bowl, add all salsa ingredients. Mix well. Set aside.

Remove skirt steak from marinade and grill for 3-5 minutes on each side or until desired doneness.

Let steak rest for 5 minutes before slicing. Serve with Peach and Avocado salsa.

honey garlic chicken

INGREDIENTS:
4 Chicken breasts
½ c. Honey
½ c. Soy sauce
  or Coconut aminos
½ c. Strawberry jam
½ c. Blackberry jam
¼ c. Hoisin Sauce
2 T. Olive oil
1 T. Garlic, minced
½ c. Onion, chopped
¼ t. Crushed red pepper flakes
1 T. Arrowroot powder
1 T. Chives
1 T. Sesame seeds

Preheat oven to 400 degrees.

Place chicken breasts in Dutch oven.

Whisk together honey, soy sauce, strawberry jam, blackberry jam, hoisin sauce, olive oil, garlic, onion, and crushed red pepper;
pour sauce over chicken.

Bake for 45 minutes or until chicken is easy to shred.

Take chicken out of Dutch oven. Shred chicken using two forks.

Transfer sauce to a saucepan. Mix together 1 T. arrowroot powder with 1 T. water and mix well. Add arrowroot powder mixture to the sauce and stir constantly until sauce thickens. Add chicken to sauce and stir well. Sprinkle on chives and sesame seeds.

honey glazed cod filets

INGREDIENTS:
1 T. Coconut oil
4 Cod filets
1 t. Ginger, minced
½ c. Honey
¼ c. Soy sauce
  or Coconut aminos
1 T. Apple cider vinegar
1 T. Sesame seed oil
½ t. Sesame seeds
½ T. Chives

In a small bowl, combine ginger, honey, soy sauce, apple cider vinegar and sesame seed oil.

Marinate cod filets in half the sauce for 10 minutes.

Heat oil in pan, add cod filets.

Cook for 5 minutes on each side.

Top with remaining sauce, chives and sesame seeds.

honey mango chicken

INGREDIENTS:

1 T, Olive oil
4 Chicken breasts, cubed
½ c. Onion, diced
1 Mango, peeled, chopped
1 c. Cashews
1 T. Garlic, minced
2 T. Soy sauce
2 T. Honey
1 T. Arrowroot powder
1 T. Water

In a large pan, heat oil. Add onion and garlic until golden brown. Add chicken and cook until chicken is no longer pink.

Add mango, cashews, soy sauce and honey. Salt and pepper to taste.

Mix arrowroot powder and water. Pour into chicken mixture and stir until sauce thickens.

korean short ribs

INGREDIENTS:

6 lbs. Short ribs
Salt
Pepper
1 medium Pear, peeled, cored and coarsely chopped
½ c. Soy sauce
  or Coconut aminos
2 T. Garlic, minced
3 Scallions, chopped
1 T. Ginger, minced
2 t. Fish sauce
1 T. Rice wine vinegar
1 c. Chicken broth
¼ c. Fresh cilantro, chopped

Preheat broiler. Liberally season short ribs with salt and pepper; lay on foil lined baking sheet. Broil ribs 5 minutes per side.

Place short ribs in a Dutch oven.

Put pear, soy sauce, garlic, scallions, ginger, fish sauce and vinegar into a food processer and blend until smooth.

Pour puree over short ribs, add broth and bake at 450 degrees for 60 minutes or until short ribs are tender.

Garnish with cilantro.

huckleberry glaze lamb chops

INGREDIENTS:

3 Lbs. Lamb chops

2 t. Garlic, minced

1/3 c. Huckleberry Syrup

2 T. Wholegrain mustard

Preheat oven to 400 degrees.

Put garlic, huckleberry syrup and mustard in a large Ziploc bag, mix well.

Add lamb chops and marinade for 1/2 hour, up to overnight.

Place lamb chops onto cookie sheet and roast about 20 minutes or until lamb is cooked as desired.

lemon tarragon scallops

INGREDIENTS:

2 Lemons, juiced
24 Scallops
1 T. Olive oil
1 T. Tarragon
1 T. Garlic, minced
2 c. Salad greens
¼ c. Sun dried tomatoes
¼ c. Pine nuts
Salt and pepper

Combine, lemon juice, olive oil, tarragon, garlic, salt and pepper.

Divide, set aside half of mixture: marinade scallops in the other half of mixture.

Sauté scallops for 3 minutes per side.

Do not over cook scallops or they will have a rubbery texture.

Serve scallops over a bed of salad greens, sun-dried tomatoes and pine nuts. Drizzle with remaining sauce.

marsala chicken

INGREDIENTS:
¼ c. Almond flour
¼ t. Salt
¼ t. Pepper
¼ t. Oregano
2 Chicken breasts
2 T. Olive oil
1 c. Mushrooms, sliced
¼ c. Marsala wine
⅛ c. Cooking sherry
½ t. Thyme

Mix almond flour, salt, pepper and oregano.

Coat chicken breasts in flour mixture.

In a large pan, heat olive oil; add chicken. Cook until chicken is no longer pink inside. Remove from pan. Set aside.

Add mushrooms, wine and cooking sherry: cover and simmer for 10 minutes.

Spoon mushrooms over chicken. Garnish with thyme.

mediterranean lamb roast

INGREDIENTS:

4 lbs. Lamb roast
1 Onion, cut into quarters
2 c. Baby carrots
2 T. Garlic, minced
½ c. Kalamata olives
32 oz. can Petite diced tomatoes

Preheat oven to 400 degrees.

Spray a Dutch oven with cooking spray.

Place all ingredients into the Dutch oven and bake for one hour or until lamb is cooked to your desired likeness and vegetables are tender.

orange chicken stir fry

INGREDIENTS:
1 Lb. Chicken breasts, diced
1 T. Coconut oil
1 large Sweet potato, diced
1 c. Carrots, matchstick
2 Stalks celery, chopped
1 c. Snap peas, chopped
Salt
Pepper
1 T. Arrowroot powder
½ c. Orange juice
2 T. Soy sauce or Coconut aminos
2 T. Rice vinegar
1 T. Fish sauce
1 t. Orange zest
2 t. Garlic, minced
1 t. Ginger, minced
1 t. Honey

In a large pan, heat coconut oil.

Add chicken, cook until chicken is no longer pink.

Add vegetables; cook until vegetables are tender.

Add salt, pepper and arrowroot powder.

In a small saucepan, add orange juice, soy sauce, rice vinegar, fish sauce, orange zest, garlic, ginger and honey.

Heat until sauce starts to thicken. Add sauce to stir-fry.

pork fried cauliflower rice

INGREDIENTS:

1 Large head cauliflower
2 Eggs
2 t. Soy sauce
  or Coconut aminos
1 T. Coconut oil
1 T. Onion, dried
1 t. Garlic, minced
1 t. Ginger, minced
1 ½ c. Broccoli, cut into florets
1 ½ c. Carrots, matchstick
2 c. Pork, cooked, cubed
2 Scallions, chopped
2 t. Sesame seeds
1 T. Hoisin sauce
2 T. Sweet chili sauce
1 t. Sesame oil

Grate cauliflower in a food processor.

Microwave the cauliflower for 2 minutes. Drain. Set aside.

Whisk eggs and soy sauce together. Scramble eggs. Set aside.

In a large pan, heat oil. Add onion, garlic, ginger, broccoli and carrots. Cook until vegetables are tender.

Add pork, cauliflower, eggs, hoisin sauce, sweet chili sauce and sesame oil.

Cook until well blended and heated through.

Sprinkle with scallions and sesame seeds.

sweet & spicy pork tenderloin

INGREDIENTS:
½ t. Cumin
½ t. Salt
¼ t. Pepper
1 t. Pumpkin pie spice
¼ t. Garlic, minced
1/8 t. Chipotle chili pepper
1 Pork tenderloin
1 t. Olive oil
2 T. Honey
1 T. Garlic, minced
1 ½ t. Hot pepper sauce

Preheat over to 350 degrees. Lightly coat roasting pan with olive oil.

In a small bowl, add cumin, salt, pepper, pumpkin pie spice, garlic and chipotle pepper. Mix well.

Rub olive oil on the tenderloin, then rub on spice mixture until evenly coated. Refrigerate for at least 15 minutes, or overnight.

Meanwhile, in a small bowl, mix honey, garlic and hot pepper sauce.

In a large pan over med-high heat, brown tenderloin in olive oil until all sides are browned. Put the tenderloin in the prepared roasting pan, spread honey, garlic mixture over the tenderloin and bake for 30 minutes or until done to your likeness. Let the tenderloin rest for 10 minutes to let the juices settle before slicing.

prosciutto wrapped chicken

INGREDIENTS:
1 T. Olive oil
1 t. Garlic, minced
4 Chicken breasts
8 Slices prosciutto
½ c. Goat cheese
½ Blueberry preserves
Salt
Pepper
Parsley

Top each chicken breast with goat cheese and blueberry preserves.

Wrap each breast with two slices of prosciutto.

In a large pan, heat oil. Add garlic, cook for 1 minute.

Add chicken breasts, season with salt, pepper and parsley. Cook until chicken is no longer pink inside.

avocado salsa salmon

INGREDIENTS:
2 lbs. Salmon filets
1 t. Olive oil
1 t. Garlic, minced
1 ½ t. Paprika
1 t. Salt
1 t. Onion, dried
½ t. Oregano
½ t. Cumin
½ t. Chili powder
½ t. Pepper
¼ t. Thyme
¼ t. Cayenne

Salsa:

1 Large avocado, seeded and diced
½ c. Grape tomatoes, sliced
1 T. Red onion, chopped finely
1 t. Lime juice
½ t. Salt
½ t. Garlic, minced
½ t. Pepper

In a small bowl, mix oil, garlic, paprika, salt, onion, oregano, cumin, chili powder, pepper, thyme and cayenne.

Rub over salmon filets.

Grill salmon for 4 minutes on both sides.

Meanwhile, mix all salsa ingredients.

Top salmon with avocado salsa.

shepard's pie

INGREDIENTS:
1 Batch mashed cauliflower (see recipe)
1 ½ T. Coconut oil
½ c. Onion, diced
2 c. Carrots, chopped
1 T. Garlic, minced
2 lbs. Ground lamb
¼ t. Salt
¼ t. Pepper
2 T. Tomato paste
1 c. Chicken broth
1 t. Soy sauce or Coconut aminos
2 t. Rosemary
1 t. Thyme
3 Egg whites
1 T. Tomato paste
¼ t. Paprika

Preheat oven to 400 degrees.

In a large pan, heat coconut oil. Add onion, garlic and carrots; cook until vegetables are tender. Remove vegetables from pan.

In the same pan, cook lamb. Add tomato paste, chicken broth, soy sauce, salt, pepper, rosemary and thyme.

Add vegetables. Simmer for 10 minutes until most of the sauce evaporates. Whisk egg whites and mix into meat mixture.Spread the meat mixture in a 9 x 13 baking dish. Spread the mashed cauliflower on top. Sprinkle with paprika.

Bake for 30 minutes until the top begins to brown.

Let shepard's pie rest for 15 minutes before serving.

shrimp & asparagus

INGREDIENTS:

1 lb. Shrimp, peeled, deveined

1 Bunch fresh asparagus, chopped

1 T. Butter

1 t. Garlic, minced

Salt

Pepper

In a pan, melt butter.

Add garlic and asparagus, cook 2 minutes.

Add shrimp, salt and pepper; cook until shrimp is cooked through.

spicy honey chicken

INGREDIENTS:

8 Chicken breasts
2 t. Olive oil
2 t. Garlic, minced
¼ t. Cayenne pepper
1 T. Onion, dried
½ t. Coriander
½ t. Salt
1 t. Cumin
½ t. Chipotle chili powder
½ c. Honey
1 T. Apple cider vinegar

In a large Ziploc bag, add garlic, cayenne, onion, coriander, salt, cumin and chipotle chili powder. Mix well.

Add chicken and refrigerate for one hour.

Meanwhile, mix honey and apple cider vinegar. Cook until well combined and heated through.

In a large pan, add Olive oil.

Sauté chicken for three minutes or until golden brown on both sides. Place chicken in a baking dish.

Pour sauce over chicken. Bake for 30-35 minutes.

stuffed pork tenderloin

INGREDIENTS:

Pork tenderloin
2 c. Spinach
⅓ c. Cashews
1 T. Garlic, minced
1 Small white onion, chopped
2 Sprigs fresh rosemary
Salt and pepper
1 T. Olive oil
½ c. Chicken broth

Preheat oven to 350 degrees.

Butterfly the tenderloin. In a food processor, combine spinach, cashews, garlic, onion, rosemary and salt and pepper.

Process until smooth. Spread mixture onto the tenderloin.

Roll up tenderloin and secure with a toothpick. In a large pan, heat oil and brown tenderloin on all sides.

Place tenderloin in a baking dish, pour chicken broth over tenderloin.

Bake for 45 minutes or until tenderloin is cooked through.

sun-dried tomato stuffed chicken

INGREDIENTS:

4 Chicken breasts

⅓ c. Sun-dried tomatoes, diced

3 ½ oz. Gorgonzola cheese, crumbled

10 Fresh sage leaves, diced

Salt

Pepper

1 T. olive oil

In a small bowl, mix together sun-dried tomatoes, gorgonzola cheese and sage.

Split chicken breasts, stuff with tomato and cheese mixture.

Sprinkle chicken breasts with salt and pepper.

Put chicken breasts in a heated pan with the olive oil and cook for 4 minutes per side, until chicken is no longer pink and cheese mixture is melted.

swedish meatballs & mushrooms

INGREDIENTS:

Meatballs:
3 Eggs
1 Onion, finely chopped
1 T. Garlic, minced
¼ c. Fresh parsley, chopped
1 t. Nutmeg
2 t. Fennel seed
2 t. Salt
2 t. Pepper
2 lbs. Ground beef
2 lbs. Ground pork sausage
4-6 T. Olive oil

Mushroom Gravy:
1 T. Butter
4 c. Mushrooms, sliced
Salt
Pepper
4 c. Beef broth
1 c. Almond milk
4 T. Water
4 T. Arrowroot powder

Meatballs: Mix all ingredients together with hands until well mixed: form into bite-sized meatballs. Cook meatballs in 2 T. olive oil in small batches, as to not crowd meatballs while browning.
Set meatballs aside.

For Gravy: In the meatball pan, add butter, mushrooms, salt and pepper and sauté until mushrooms are cooked.

Add almond milk and broth, heat until boiling.

In a small bowl, stir together water and arrowroot powder until smooth. Pour into pan and cook until gravy thickens.

Pour gravy over meatballs and serve.

sweet chili pork chops & pears

INGREDIENTS:
1 T. Olive oil
2 Pears, peeled, cored and diced
1 T. Onion, dried
¼ c. Sweet chili sauce
1 t. Ginger, minced
1 t. Garlic, minced
½ c. Soy sauce
  or Coconut aminos
Salt
Pepper

Season pork chops with salt and pepper on both sides.

In large pan, heat olive oil. Cook pork chops for 4 minutes on each side.

Remove from pan. Set aside and keep warm.

In the large pan, add onions, garlic, ginger and pears. Cook until tender.

Add sweet chili sauce and soy sauce.

Pour pear and onion mixture over pork chops.

sweet potato bake

INGREDIENTS:
1 lb. Ground sausage
¼ c. Coconut oil
1 t. Chili powder
2 t. Cumin
¼ t. Cinnamon
1 t. Ground ginger
3 T. Curry powder
½ Onion, chopped
1 T. Garlic, minced
2 Apples, chopped
2 c. Fresh spinach, chopped
Salt
Pepper
½ t. Cilantro
3 Sweet potatoes, chopped

In a large pan, brown sausage. Remove from pan.

In the same large pan, add onions and garlic: cook until tender.

Add sweet potatoes, apples, chili powder, cumin, cinnamon, ginger, curry, salt and pepper.

Cook until sweet potatoes are tender.

Add sausage, spinach and cilantro. Heat through.

sweet potato turkey burgers

INGREDIENTS:

1 lb. Ground turkey

1 c. Mashed sweet potato

¼ c. Onions, finely chopped

1 t. Garlic, minced

¼ c. Fresh cilantro, chopped

1 Egg, beaten

1 t. Salt

1 t. Pepper

1 t. Cumin

1 t. Cinnamon

1 t. Hot chili sauce

Mix all ingredients and divide into ½ cup portions and pound into patties.

Cook in a pan on medium heat with 1 T. olive oil, for approximately 5 minutes per side.

tomato basil chicken

INGREDIENTS:
4 Chicken breasts
1 - 15 oz. can Petite diced tomatoes
½ c. Sundried tomatoes, chopped
¼ c. Onion, chopped
1 T. Garlic, minced
½ t. Oregano
½ c. Fresh basil, chopped
Salt
Pepper

Season chicken with salt and pepper.

Grill chicken for 5 minutes on both sides.

In a small saucepan, add all remaining ingredients and cook until heated through.

Remove chicken from grill and top with tomato basil sauce.

turkey stir fry

INGREDIENTS:

2 lb. Ground turkey
1 T. Coconut oil
1 T. Garlic, minced
1 T. Ginger, minced
2 c. Carrots, matchstick
2 c. Bean sprouts
½ c. Hoisin sauce
½ c. Sweet chili sauce
½ t. Fish sauce
1 Bunch cilantro, chopped
½ c. Cashews, chopped

In a medium pan, heat oil.

Add garlic, ginger and turkey. Cook until turkey is no longer pink.

Add carrots, bean sprouts, hoisin sauce, sweet chili sauce and fish sauce. Cook until vegetables are tender.

Top with cashews and cilantro.

basil mayo veal

INGREDIENTS:

1 T. Olive oil
2 t. Garlic, minced
8 Veal Cutlets
8 Slices prosciutto
1 c. Mayo
1 c. Sundried tomatoes
1 c. Basil, chopped

In a large Pan, heat olive oil, add garlic.

Mix sun-dried tomatoes, 1/4 c. basil; divide among veal cutlets.

Roll cutlets, wrap in prosciutto.

Secure with a toothpick. Cook cutlets until golden brown on
each side.

Meanwhile, mix remaining basil with the mayo.

Remove cutlets from pan and top with basil mayo.

desserts

apple crisp

INGREDIENTS:

6 Apples, peeled, cored and sliced
2 T. Tapioca
2 T. Coconut sugar
1 t. Cinnamon
1 t. Vanilla

Crumble:
2 c. Almond flour
2 T. Coconut sugar
1 t. Xanthan gum
½ c. Butter
½ c. Almonds, sliced

Preheat oven to 400 degrees.

Butter a 9x13-baking dish.

In a large bowl, combine apples, tapioca, sugar, cinnamon and vanilla. Add apples to the baking dish.

In a medium bowl, combine almond flour, sugar, xanthan gum and butter. Mix well.

Crumble mixture over apples. Sprinkle with almonds.

Bake for 45 minutes or until apples are tender and topping is golden brown.

berries & whipped coconut cream

INGREDIENTS:

1 14.5 oz. can Coconut milk, chilled

2 c. Fresh berries: strawberries, raspberries and blueberries

1 t. Almond or vanilla extract

2 T. Sliced almonds

Open the can of coconut milk from the bottom; pour off any liquid that has separated. Scoop the thickened coconut milk into a mixing bowl, add the almond or vanilla extract and whip until the coconut milk becomes fluffy.

Put berries into individual serving dishes. Scoop the whipped coconut milk onto the berries. Top with sliced almonds.

brownie bites

INGREDIENTS:
2/3 c. Walnuts, chopped
1/3 c. Cocoa powder
1½ c. Medjool dates, pitted
1 T. Vanilla extract
1 ½ T Coconut milk
2/3 c. Coconut, shredded

Place dates in a bowl of warm water to soften them. Drain.
Add all ingredients in a food processor, pulse until well combined.

Refrigerate for 2 hours.

Roll dough into balls and roll in cocoa powder.

coconut meltaways

INGREDIENTS:

1 ½ c. Almond flour
2 c. Coconut, shredded
1/3 c. Coconut flour
½ t. Salt
½ c. Maple syrup
4 T. Lemon juice
2 T. Vanilla
1 T. Lemon zest
1 T. Coconut oil, melted

In a small bowl, combine almond flour, coconut, coconut flour and salt. Set aside.

In a medium bowl, combine maple syrup, lemon juice, vanilla and lemon zest. Add dry ingredient mixture to the wet ingredients; add 1 T. melted coconut oil.

Using a cookie scoop, scoop dough and roll into balls. Place on cookie sheet.

Bake cookies at 200 degrees for 45 minutes.

coconut flour crepes

INGREDIENTS:

6 Eggs

1 t. Coconut oil, melted

½ t. Vanilla

1 T. Coconut cream, unsweetened

1 t. Honey

4 T. Coconut flour

In a small bowl, combine eggs, coconut oil, vanilla, coconut cream and honey. Whisk until fluffy.

Add coconut flour and mix well. The batter should be very thin.

Using a crepe pan, dip pan in batter and cook. I usually always lose my first crepe of every batch. It seems like that first crepe gets the pan ready.

Fill crepes with fresh berries and top with fresh whipped cream.

coconut macaroons

INGREDIENTS:

2 egg whites, beaten, at room temperature

2 T. Honey

¼ t. Salt

Zest of one lemon (approx. 1 tablespoon)

1 t. Vanilla extract

2 c. Coconut, shredded

Preheat oven to 325 degrees.

Line a baking sheet with parchment paper. Set aside.

In a large bowl, whisk egg whites, honey and salt until well combined and frothy. Whisk in lemon zest and vanilla, just to combine. Add in coconut and stir until it is well coated by the egg white mixture.

Using a cookie scoop, scoop mixture and drop onto the baking sheet.

Bake 15-20 minutes, or until golden brown, rotating halfway through.

Place baking sheet on a cooling rack and allow macaroons to cool.

flourless chocolate cake

INGREDIENTS:

16 oz. Semi sweet chocolate chips
1 c. Butter
4 Eggs, separated
1 c. Coconut Sugar
¾ t. Cream of tarter

Topping:
¾ c. Chocolate chips
2 T. Butter, melted
1 T. Honey
¼ t. Vanilla
½ c. Pecans, chopped

Preheat oven to 325 degrees. Line the bottom of a spring form pan with parchment paper. Set aside. In a small microwave safe bowl, add chocolate chips and butter, melt. Set aside. In a small bowl, beat egg yolks and coconut sugar. Add egg yolks to chocolate mixture and mix well.

In a large bowl, beat egg whites with the cream of tarter until stiff. Fold egg whites into chocolate mixture. Pour batter into spring form pan. Bake for 30 minutes, or until toothpick inserted into cake comes out clean.

Topping:

In a small saucepan, add chocolate chips, butter, honey and vanilla. Cook until melted. Pour chocolate over cooled cake. Sprinkle with pecans. Enjoy with a dollop of fresh whipped cream.

flourless zucchini brownies

INGREDIENTS:
1 ¼ c. Finely grated Zucchini
1 ¼ c. Almond butter
¾ c. Honey
½ T. Vanilla
1 t. Baking soda
¼ c. Cocoa powder
¼ c. Milk chocolate chips
1 Egg
dash Salt

Preheat oven to 350 degrees. Place grated zucchini in a paper towel to remove excess water.

Mix all ingredients in a large bowl. Stir until well mixed.

Line a 9x9 baking dish with parchment paper. Spray parchment paper with coconut oil spray.

Pour batter in pan and smooth using a plastic spatula.

Bake for 15-20 minutes or until a toothpick comes out clean.

Do not over bake as the brownies will become very dry.

fresh blueberry crumble

INGREDIENTS:
2 pints Fresh blueberries
1 T. Lemon juice
2 c. Almond flour
½ c. Macadamia nuts, chopped
½ c Butter, melted
½ t. Maple syrup
1 t. Cinnamon
½ t. Salt

Preheat oven to 375 degrees. Butter a 9x13-baking dish.

In a medium bowl, place blueberries and lemon juice. Mix well. Pour berries into the baking dish.

In a medium bowl, mix flour, macadamia nuts, butter, maple syrup, cinnamon and salt. Sprinkle over the berries. Bake for
30-40 minutes or until topping is golden brown.

mocha bacon brownies

INGREDIENTS:

8 oz. Dark chocolate, melted, cooled

1 c. Butter, melted, cooled

1 c. Maple syrup

6 Eggs

2 T. Cocoa powder

4 T. Instant coffee

4 Slices bacon, cooked, crumbled

Preheat oven to 375 degrees.

Line a 9x13-baking dish with parchment paper. Set aside.

In a medium bowl, add chocolate, butter, maple syrup and eggs; mix well. Slowly whisk in cocoa powder and coffee.

Pour batter into baking dish. Bake for 30 minutes or until a toothpick inserted comes out clean.

Sprinkle the bacon on top for the last 15 minutes of baking.

peanut butter cookies

INGREDIENTS:

1 c. Peanut Butter

1 c. Coconut sugar

1 Egg, beaten

1 t. Vanilla

Preheat oven to 325 degrees.

Mix all ingredients.

Drop cookie dough by spoonfuls onto an ungreased baking sheet. Depress a fork onto each cookie, creating a crosshatch pattern.

Bake for 8-10 minutes.

pear crisp

INGREDIENTS:
2 c. Almond flour
½ t. Xanthan gum
½ c. Macadamia nuts, chopped
½ c. Butter
1 t. Honey
1 t. Cinnamon
½ t. Salt
5 Ripe pears, peeled, cored, sliced
1 T. Tapioca
1 T. Honey

Preheat oven to 350 degrees. Butter an 8 x 8 pan.

In a small bowl, mix almond flour, xanthan gum, macadamia nuts, butter, honey, cinnamon, and salt. Mix well. Set aside.

In a medium bowl, mix pears, tapioca and honey.

Put pears in the baking dish and crumble flour mixture on top.

Bake for 40 or until pears are tender and crumble is golden brown.

pineapple whip

INGREDIENTS:

2 c. Pineapple, frozen

1 c. Coconut milk

In a blender, combine ingredients and blend well.

pumpkin crumble bars

INGREDIENTS:

⅔ c. Coconut flour
4 t. Pumpkin pie spice
2 t. Cinnamon
¼ t. Salt
4 Eggs, beaten
⅔ c. Pumpkin puree
⅔ c. Maple syrup
½ c. Almond milk
¼ c. Butter, melted
2 t. Vanilla extract
1 t. Baking soda
2 t. Apple cider vinegar

Crumble topping:
⅔ c. Almond flour
½ c. Coconut, shredded
2 T. Coconut sugar
½ t. Cinnamon
5 T. Butter, melted

Preheat oven 350 degrees. Butter a 9x13-baking dish. Set aside.

In a large bowl, combine flour, pumpkin pie spice, cinnamon and salt. Mix well. Set aside.

In a large bowl, mix eggs, almond milk, pumpkin, butter, maple syrup and vanilla. Mix well.

In a small bowl, mix baking soda and apple cider vinegar. Add mixture to the egg mixture. Add flour mixture to the egg mixture. Mix well. Pour batter into the baking dish.

In a medium bowl, using a fork, combine all topping ingredients. Crumble the topping mixture onto the batter. Bake for 28-30 minutes or until topping is golden brown and a toothpick inserted into the batter comes out clean. Cool completely before cutting.

pumpkin pie custard

INGREDIENTS:
1 c. Pumpkin puree
2 t. Pumpkin pie spice
Pinch of salt
2 Eggs, beaten
¼ c. Maple syrup
1 t. Vanilla
1 c. Coconut milk

Preheat oven to 350 degrees.

Boil 4 cups of water.

In a small bowl, combine all ingredients.

Pour custard into small ramekins.

Place the ramekins onto a baking dish and pour boiling water into baking dish, enough water to come up halfway to the top of the ramekins. Be careful not to get any of the boiling water into the ramekins.

Bake for 45-60 minutes or until a knife inserted into the center of the custard comes out clean.

Serve with a dollop of fresh whipped cream.

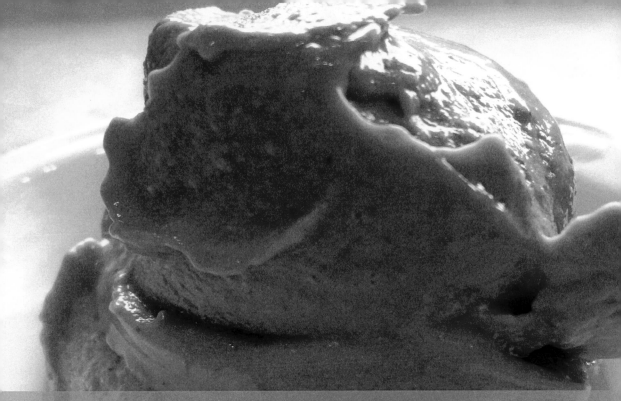

raspberry "ice cream"

INGREDIENTS:
1 c. Bananas, sliced, frozen
1 c. Raspberries, frozen
½ c. Coconut cream
½ c. Almond milk
¼ t. Vanilla

In a blender, mix all ingredients.

Made in the USA
San Bernardino, CA
01 April 2016